Control Your TIME Or STAY STUCK You Choose

By

Adam Fox
©adamfox2025

© 2025 Adam Fox

All rights reserved. This book or any portion thereof may not be reproduced, distributed, or transmitted in any form or by any means, including photocopying, recording, or other electronic or mechanical methods, without the prior written permission of the author, except for brief quotations in a book review or critical article.

The scanning, uploading, and distribution of this book via the Internet or via any other means without the permission of the publisher is illegal and punishable by law. Please purchase only authorised electronic editions, and do not participate in or encourage electronic piracy of copyrighted materials. Your support of the author's rights is appreciated.

For permission requests, contact the author:

Adam Fox

adam@evolvebusinesscoaching.co.uk

www. evolvebusinesscoaching.co.uk

First Edition

Publisher's Note: This book is a work of nonfiction. While the author has made every effort to ensure the accuracy and completeness of the information contained in this book, the author assumes no responsibility for errors, omissions, or contrary interpretations of the subject matter herein.

ISBN: 9798282345940

Table of Contents

Foreword	1
Why You Need This Book	5
Chapter 1:	7
Time is Your Most Limited Resource—Stop Wasting It	
Chapter 2:	23
The Productivity Myth	
Why Working Harder is Holding You Back	
Chapter 3:	42
Flawed Productivity Advice – Why Most Productivity Tips Don't Work	
Chapter 4:	59
Finding Your Focus –	
Time Blocking or The Daily Big Three?	
Chapter 5:	85
The Psychology of Procrastination –	
Why You're Your Own Worst Enemy	
Chapter 6:	106
Understanding Your Own Brain & Natural Productivity Rhythms	
Chapter 7:	131
Brain Dumping	
Clearing Mental Clutter to Get More Done	
Chapter 8:	150
The DROP System	
Chapter 9:	166
Protecting Your Time	
Appendix 1:	181
Additional Resources and Tools	181
Appendix 2:	187
Further Reading Recommendations	187
Appendix 3: Acknowledgements And Bibliography	192

Bibliography & References	194
About the Author	197
Services Offered by the Author	201
Contact Details	205
One More Thing Before You Go…	206

Foreword

I never set out to be an author. Hell, I barely scraped through GCSE English, and the thought of writing anything longer than my name used to make my skin crawl. But life has a way of forcing you out of your comfort zone.

For years, I was the guy who thought working harder was the answer. I wore long hours like a badge of honour, convinced that success was just on the other side of one more late night, one more packed schedule, one more sacrifice.

But it never was.

Instead, I found myself constantly stressed, stretched too thin, and missing out on the very things that actually mattered. My brain was always running through unfinished tasks, unanswered emails, forgotten commitments, and that all-too-familiar 2 AM "Oh shit, I forgot to do that!" moment, where I'd email myself in the middle of the night just so I wouldn't forget in the morning.

The irony? I wasn't lazy. I wasn't slacking. I was busting my arse and still feeling like I was always behind.

So, I did what most people do—I went looking for answers. I read every productivity book I could get my hands on. I tested every method, system, and so-called "hack." I studied psychology, neuroscience, time management frameworks, and discipline techniques. I went all in on figuring out what actually works.

And here's what I realised: Most of the advice out there is complete rubbish.

- "Just wake up at 5 AM!" – Great advice… if you're a morning person. If you're not, it's just self-inflicted torture.
- "Hustle harder!" – No thanks, already tried that, and it nearly wrecked me.
- "Follow this one-size-fits-all system, and you'll be successful!" – Nonsense. Productivity isn't universal—it's personal.

The truth is, being productive isn't about doing more—it's about doing less of the wrong things. It's about clearing your mental load, cutting through the noise, and focusing on what actually moves the needle. It's about creating time for what matters most—not just working yourself into the ground.

For me, that meant becoming a fully present husband and father while still doing something I love. It meant making sure my time was optimised so I could have the best of everything—a successful business, meaningful work, and time to actually enjoy life with my family.

But this book isn't about me.

This book is about you.

Because if you're anything like I was, you're drowning in work, fighting to keep up, and feeling like no matter how hard you push, there's never enough time. You wake up already behind. You go to bed exhausted but still wondering what the hell you actually accomplished. You've tried the "systems," the planners, the apps, the motivational quotes, but nothing sticks.

You don't need more time—you need a better way to use it.

This Book is Different

This isn't a book about hustle culture or waking up at 5 AM to "win the day."

It's not about adding more to your plate or squeezing every last second out of your schedule.

It's about cutting the crap.

- Stopping the chaos.
- Reclaiming your time.
- Building a system that works for you—not against you.

This book exists to save you the years of frustration, trial and error, and wasted effort that I went through. This is to help you take control of your time so you can stop grinding and start actually living.

Because if you win, I win.

And that's my goal—to help as many people as possible break free from the overwhelm, the distractions, and the constant battle with time.

This Book is a Tool—Use It.

This isn't something you read once and forget about. It's a playbook—a reference you can return to whenever you need clarity, focus, or a kick up the backside.

- Scribble in it.
- Highlight the parts that hit home.
- Use the exercises to implement real change.

Most importantly, commit to taking action. Because while this book can guide you, only you can make the decision to take control of your time, your business, and your life.

Acknowledgements

I couldn't have written this without the people who've shaped me along the way.

To my wife, Danielle—You've been my anchor for the last 16 years. Your love and support mean everything, and I couldn't have done this without you.

To my daughters, Charlotte and Amelia—You've taught me what balance really means. Watching you grow has inspired me to lead by example—not just in business but in life.

To Alan Brighton, my first coach—You tore down my limiting beliefs and rebuilt me as a stronger leader. Thank you for lighting the path that led me here.

To every client who's trusted me with their business and their challenges—You've shown me that transformation isn't just possible; it's inevitable when you commit to doing the work.

This book is for you.

Why You Need This Book

Right now, you probably feel like you're drowning.

Your **to-do list never ends.** Your inbox is out of control. There's always **someone demanding your time—your boss, your employees, your clients, your family.**

You wake up already behind.

You finish the day exhausted but still feel like you've accomplished nothing.

You know you **need more time**, but no matter how much you push yourself, there's never enough.

Sound familiar?

You're not the problem. The way you've been taught to manage your time is.

- You've been told that being "busy" is the same as being productive. **It's not.**
- You've been told that working harder will fix it. **It won't.**
- You've been told that time management is about cramming more in. **That's wrong.**

This book is different. It's not here to tell you to wake up earlier, hustle harder, or micromanage every second of your day. **It's here to show you how to take back control.**

With the strategies in this book, you'll learn how to:

- **Stop feeling overwhelmed by endless tasks and distractions.**
- **Finally, get your important work done without working any longer.**
- **Take control of your schedule instead of letting others dictate it.**
- **Create time for what actually matters to YOU.**

And most importantly, you'll learn how to **protect** that time—so you don't just fill it with more pointless tasks, meetings, and demands from everyone else.

If you're tired of feeling like you're always behind, this book is your way out.

Because time is the one thing you can never get back. Let's make sure you start using it wisely.

Now, let's get to work.

Chapter 1: Time is Your Most Limited Resource—Stop Wasting It

Section 1: The Hard Truth About Time

Let's get one thing straight—your time is running out.

And no, that's not me trying to be dramatic. It's just the cold, hard truth that most people spend their lives ignoring.

You don't have unlimited time. You never did. You are spending it every second of every day, whether you like it or not. The question is: Are you spending it on things that actually matter, or are you just filling your days with bullshit?

Most people aren't honest about this.

They tell themselves they'll "make time" for the important stuff later—when work isn't so busy, when they've made more money, and when life isn't so chaotic.

But here's the problem with "later"... it never fucking comes.

We live under this delusion that time is infinite. That we have all the time in the world to work, to build, to love, to enjoy. That we'll retire at 65 and finally start living.

But here's a reality check: Some people never make it to retirement. Some people don't even make it to next year.

Oliver Burkeman's *Four Thousand Weeks* puts it into perspective:

The average human lifespan is around 4,000 weeks.

That's it. Four thousand Mondays. Four thousand Sundays.

And unless you're still in your teens (which you probably aren't if you're reading this book), a big chunk of those weeks are already gone.

Let me ask you something:

- How many of those weeks have you actually lived?
- How many did you waste on things that don't matter?
- How many do you have left, and what the hell are you going to do with them?

If your answer is "I don't know" or "I'll figure it out later", you need this book more than you think.

Now, I'm not telling you this to send you into an existential crisis. The point isn't to sit around panicking about the passage of time—it's to do something about it.

And that doesn't mean filling every spare second with work.

That's the lie hustle culture has been selling you. The idea is that if you could just be more productive, work harder, and grind 24/7, you'd finally have enough time.

No.

Productivity isn't about cramming more in.

It's about reclaiming your time so you can actually live.

Here's the kicker: More time doesn't fix anything if you don't use it wisely.

Most people who "gain extra hours" just fill them with more of the same—more pointless meetings, more scrolling, more distractions, more time wasted.

What if, instead, you actually did less?

- More time with your family.
- More time doing the things you love.
- More time to just exist—without guilt.

The goal of this book isn't to help you work harder.

The goal of this book is to help you stop wasting time on the wrong things so you can spend more time on what actually matters.

- You want a thriving business? You need time to build it.
- You want more freedom? You need time to enjoy it.
- You want to be present with your kids? You need to stop burning through time on pointless tasks that don't move the needle.

The problem isn't that you don't have enough time.

The problem is that you're spending it on the wrong things.

So, let's fix that.

Because you **can't** control how much time you have left.

But you **CAN** control how you use it.

And that starts right now.

Section 2: The One Goal We All Share

It doesn't matter who you are, what you do for a living, or what your day-to-day looks like.

You want more time.

That's why you picked up this book.

Maybe you haven't realised it yet, but that's the one thing you have in common with every other person reading these pages—the relentless need for more time.

It doesn't matter if you're a CEO, a freelancer, a stay-at-home parent, or an employee stuck in the middle of the corporate machine—you constantly feel like you don't have enough hours in the day to do everything you need to do.

And here's the kicker: you never will.

Not if you keep running on the same broken system that's keeping you stuck.

Because here's the problem—society has convinced you that being constantly busy is normal. That you should be hustling, grinding, working, achieving, and filling every waking second with something productive.

It's bullshit.

The world has tricked you into believing that your time is infinite—that you can always "get to it later." That someday, you'll finally have time for yourself, time to breathe, time to do all the things you keep putting off.

But let me ask you something: When was the last time you truly felt like you had enough time?

- CEOs feel like their schedules own them. Endless meetings, back-to-back calls, and a flood of emails mean they're "busy," but when do they actually get time to think? To strategise? To enjoy the success they've worked so hard for?
- Business owners dream of freedom, but instead, they find themselves trapped in their own businesses—working longer hours than they ever did in a job, constantly firefighting, wondering when they'll finally be able to step back.
- Middle managers are stuck in the worst of both worlds—squeezed between the demands from the top and the needs of their teams. No time to focus, no time to get ahead, and no time to stop feeling like they're being pulled in a hundred different directions.
- Solopreneurs thought working for themselves would mean freedom. Instead, they're doing everything—marketing, admin, sales, delivery—while never truly switching off.
- Stay-at-home parents? Forget about time. If they get five minutes to drink a coffee while it's still hot, it's a miracle. Every second of the day is spent juggling kids, chores, errands, and a to-do list that never seems to shrink.

Different lives. Different responsibilities. Same fundamental problem.

No one feels like they have enough time.

And it's because most people don't even realise how much time they're wasting on the wrong things.

Every day, you spend time:

- Reacting instead of planning, jumping from one urgent task to the next, and never getting ahead.
- Saying yes to things that don't matter: meetings, obligations, favours that add nothing to your life.
- Trying to do everything yourself instead of delegating or automating.
- Drowning in distractions: emails, social media, pointless conversations that steal hours of your day.

And the worst part? You think this is just how life is.

You think if you just work a little harder, wake up a little earlier, or get a little more organised, you'll finally find the time you're looking for.

You won't.

The solution isn't to do more; it's to do less of the wrong things so you can free up time for the right ones.

That's why this book exists.

This isn't about squeezing every last drop of energy out of your day just to get more shit done.

It's about learning how to cut through the noise, eliminate the pointless crap, and focus on what actually moves the needle—so you can finally get your time back.

Maybe that means working fewer hours while making more money.

Maybe that means finally having time to exercise, or travel, or just sit the hell down and breathe.

Maybe that means stepping back from the never-ending grind and actually enjoying life.

Whatever your version of success looks like, you need time to make it happen.

If you don't get ruthless about how you use your time, the world will keep stealing it from you.

- Work will take it.
- Other people will take it.
- Your own bad habits will take it.

And before you know it, you'll wake up one day realising you spent your entire life waiting for "someday" to arrive.

So here's the deal:

You can either take control of your time now, or you can keep watching it disappear.

This book is going to show you how to take it back—permanently.

Because time isn't something you can earn back later.

You either use it wisely now, or you lose it forever.

Section 3: Who This Book is For

This book isn't just for business owners or CEOs. It's not just for entrepreneurs or freelancers trying to claw back their work-life balance. It's for anyone who has ever thought, "There just aren't enough hours in the day."

Because here's the thing—everyone wants more time.

It doesn't matter what you do for a living or where you are in life. The one universal struggle that unites all of us is that we're all running out of time, and most of us don't know how to get it back.

But here's where people go wrong: they assume that time management is just a business problem. That productivity is something only "busy professionals" need to care about.

That's complete bullshit.

Time management is a life skill. If you don't learn how to control your time, you're not just going to struggle at work—you're going to struggle in every aspect of your life.

Because time isn't just about work.

It's about freedom.

It's about choices.

It's about making sure you don't get to the end of your life thinking, "Shit, I wasted it."

That's why this book is for:

1. The Business Owners Who Thought They'd Have More Freedom

- You started your own business because you wanted to be in control of your time.
- Instead, you work longer hours than you ever did in a job.
- You're constantly firefighting, never switching off, and wondering when the hell you're actually going to enjoy the life you were supposed to be building.

2. The CEOs and Senior Leaders Who Feel Trapped by Their Own Success

- You worked your arse off to get to the top—so why does it feel like you have less time now than ever?
- You spend all day in meetings, answering emails, dealing with other people's problems, and by the time you actually sit down to do your own work, it's already 7 p.m.
- Your calendar is full, your to-do list is endless, and no matter how much you get done, it never feels like enough.

3. The Middle Managers Stuck in the Shitstorm Between the Top and Bottom

- Your boss expects you to handle everything, your team needs constant support, and you're juggling so many responsibilities that you don't even know what your actual job is anymore.
- You're stuck in back-to-back meetings all day, which means your "real work" starts after 5 p.m.

- You feel like you're constantly working, constantly catching up, and constantly exhausted.

4. The Solopreneurs Who Have No One to Blame But Themselves

- You quit your job to be your own boss, and now? You're working for a lunatic—you.
- You're doing everything—admin, marketing, sales, delivery, bookkeeping—because you feel like you "can't afford" to outsource.
- You're always working, never switching off, and constantly stuck in survival mode.

5. The Employees Who Feel Like Work is Slowly Eating Their Lives

- You start work at nine and finish at five, but somehow… your brain never stops.
- Even when you're not working, you're still checking emails, responding to messages, and stressing about your workload.
- You feel like you never truly switch off, and even when you're "relaxing," you can't shake the guilt that you should be doing something productive.

6. The Stay-at-Home Parents Who Never Get a Break

- You don't have a "job," but your workload is bigger than most full-time employees.
- Your day is a non-stop cycle of housework, childcare, errands, and zero time for yourself.
- You spend every second looking after everyone else, and by the time you finally get a minute to yourself, you're too exhausted to do anything.

Different situations, same result: your time is slipping away, and you don't know how to take it back.

So, let's make one thing clear—this book is not about working harder. It's not about squeezing more hours out of your day just so you can be more "productive" in the traditional sense.

It's about finally taking control of your time so you can live on your own terms.

It's about learning how to:

- Cut the crap that wastes your time.
- Prioritise what actually matters.
- Work smarter, not longer.
- Stop feeling like your time belongs to everyone but you.

Because no matter who you are or what you do, the goal is the same: You want more time to live.

And if you don't learn how to manage it now, you'll wake up one day and realise it's already gone.

Section 4: Why Productivity Isn't About Doing More

Let's talk about the biggest misconception around productivity: the idea that being productive means doing more. More work, more tasks, more output, more hours.

That's what we've all been led to believe, right? That success belongs to the people who outwork, out-hustle and out-grind everyone else. The ones who wake up at 5 AM, power through 16-hour days, and wear their exhaustion like a badge of honour.

But let me ask you this—if working harder was the answer, wouldn't every nurse, teacher, and construction worker be a millionaire? Wouldn't the people pulling 60-hour weeks be the ones living the dream?

They're not. And that's because working harder is not the same as working smarter.

The real goal of productivity isn't to find new ways to cram more into your already packed day—it's to get the right things done faster so you can spend more time doing what actually matters to you.

That's where most people go wrong. They focus on being busy, not being effective.

So before we go any further, let's redefine what productivity actually means—because if you don't get this part right, you'll spend your whole life working your arse off and still feel like you're never making progress.

The Difference Between Being Busy and Being Productive

Ever had one of those days where you were flat out from morning till night, running around like a headless chicken, but at the end of it, you still felt like you achieved nothing?

That's because busyness and productivity are not the same thing.

- **Busy people** fill their time with low-value tasks, jumping from one thing to the next with no real strategy.
- **Productive people** focus on what actually moves the needle, cutting out the distractions and getting the important stuff done as efficiently as possible.

Here's what that looks like in practice:

The key takeaway? The goal isn't to do more—it's to do less, better.

Busy People	Productive People
Say yes to every meeting	Question if a meeting is necessary before agreeing to it
Work long hours	Work focused hours
Keep long to-do lists with 20+ tasks	Prioritise 3–5 key tasks per day
Answer emails as they come in	Batch emails and limit unnecessary replies
Get stuck in perfectionism	Focus on progress over perfection

And that starts with understanding the real purpose of productivity.

The Real Reason You Need to Be More Productive

Most people assume productivity is about getting ahead at work, hitting deadlines, climbing the career ladder, or making more money.

That's not what this book is about.

Because here's the truth—you don't need to be more productive for the sake of work. You need to be more productive for the sake of your life.

Being more productive isn't about squeezing more work into your day.

It's about freeing yourself from the endless cycle of busy work so you can have more time for the things that actually matter.

That could mean:

- Finishing work earlier so you can spend time with your family.
- Getting the important stuff done in less time so you're not working late every night.
- Making your business more efficient so you can actually step away from it.
- Finally, having time for the hobbies, travel, and relaxation, you keep putting off.

Because the whole point of productivity isn't to work more—it's to work less while still getting the results you need.

And if you can get the same amount done in half the time? That's real success.

Why Most Productivity Advice is Garbage

At this point, you might be thinking, "Alright, I get it. I need to work smarter, not harder. But how?"

And that's where things get tricky—because most of the productivity advice out there is complete crap.

If you've ever tried following mainstream productivity advice, you've probably heard things like:

- "Wake up at 5 AM as successful people do."
- "Just stop procrastinating and get to work."
- "Hustle harder and sleep less."

And guess what? None of that actually helps.

- Waking up at 5 AM is useless if you're a night owl and can't function before noon.
- Telling someone to "just stop procrastinating" is like telling someone with anxiety to "just relax."

- Hustling harder doesn't guarantee results—it just guarantees burnout.

The problem is that most productivity advice tries to force everyone into a one-size-fits-all system. But real productivity isn't about following someone else's routine—it's about finding what works for you.

That's what this book is here to help you do.

You're not going to get a list of rigid rules to follow. You're going to get strategies you can adapt to fit your own life, energy levels, and goals.

Because the ultimate goal of productivity isn't about being "better at work." It's about getting your time back.

The Big Shift: From Workhorse to Strategist

If you take nothing else from this chapter, remember this:

Your value isn't in how much time you spend working. It's in the results you produce.

Think of it like this:

- **A workhorse** pulls the plough all day, grinding out hour after hour, never stopping, never questioning.
- **A strategist** finds the best way to get the work done in the shortest amount of time—maybe by using a better tool, delegating the task, or just eliminating the work entirely.

Who do you think is more valuable?

The business owner who works 80-hour weeks, doing everything themselves, micromanaging every little detail?

Or the business owner who works 20 hours a week, has a streamlined system, an efficient team, and plenty of free time to enjoy life?

The difference isn't hard work—it's smart work.

And that's what this book is going to help you master.

You don't need to work harder—you need to work better.

You don't need to do more—you need to do less of the wrong things.

You don't need more time—you need to start using the time you already have properly.

And if you're ready to do that, then you're exactly where you need to be.

Now, let's talk about how this book is going to change the way you work, think, and manage your time—for good.

Section 5: What's Next?

By now, you should have one thing drilled into your brain: time is your most valuable resource, and you've been wasting too much of it.

The good news? That changes now.

But before we dive into the practical stuff, there's one final concept you need to accept: **you are never getting to the end of your to-do list.**

I know that might sound depressing, but it's actually liberating.

Think about it.

Have you ever had a day where you finished every single task, cleared your inbox to zero, and sat back thinking, "That's it? I'm done. Nothing else to do."

Of course not. Because the more you get done, the more you're expected to do.

- You smash through your tasks at work? You get given more.
- You reply to every email? Your inbox fills up again within minutes.
- You tick off every task today? Guess what? There's a fresh batch waiting for you tomorrow.

It never ends.

So, let's get something straight—productivity isn't about doing more. It's about choosing what **NOT** to do.

This is where most people go wrong. They assume that if they just work harder, manage their time better, and get more efficient, they'll finally "catch up."

You won't.

There will always be more work, more tasks, more expectations, and more demands on your time.

The secret to real productivity isn't about squeezing more in—it's about getting ruthless about what makes the cut and what gets ignored.

The Power of Not Doing Things

Most productivity books focus on what you should do—how to get through your tasks faster, how to prioritise better, and how to manage your workload more efficiently.

This book is about something far more important: what you should choose **NOT** to do.

Because the truth is, most of the stuff on your to-do list doesn't actually matter.

It feels urgent. It feels important. But in reality? It's just noise.

The key to taking back control of your time isn't just about getting things done—it's about actively cutting out the crap that's clogging up your day.

This means:

- Deleting tasks that don't move the needle.
- Saying no to meetings that don't need to happen.
- Not responding to emails that don't require your input.
- Letting go of the idea that you have to "do it all."

The real game-changer isn't about getting better at time management—it's about learning to ignore the right things.

Offensive vs Defensive Time Management

Most people operate in defensive mode when it comes to their time.

- They react to emails as they come in.
- They jump from one task to the next based on what feels urgent.
- They let their schedules be dictated by other people's demands.

That's why they feel like they're constantly drowning in work.

This book is going to teach you how to flip the script and go on the offensive.

- Instead of reacting to your inbox, you'll control when you deal with emails.
- Instead of letting other people steal your time, you'll learn how to protect it.
- Instead of trying to "get through" everything, you'll learn how to ignore the 80% that doesn't matter and focus on the 20% that does.

This is about taking control, not just keeping up.

Because real productivity isn't about working harder—it's about setting the rules for how you use your time and sticking to them.

What You Can Expect from This Book

Over the next chapters, we're going to break down everything you need to know to take control of your time, including:

1. **The Productivity Myths That Are Keeping You Stuck**
   - Why everything you've been told about "working harder" is complete nonsense.
   - The difference between being busy and being productive—and why most people get it wrong.

2. **How to Design a Productivity System That Works for YOU**
   - Why copying someone else's routine never works.
   - How to figure out your own natural energy patterns so you can work at your best.
   - The key habits and tools that will help you get more done in less time.

3. **How to Stop Procrastinating and Actually Get Stuff Done**
    - The real reason you put things off (spoiler: it's not just laziness).
    - How to trick your brain into taking action—even when you don't feel motivated.
4. **The Time-Blocking System That Will Change the Way You Work**
    - How to schedule your day around your energy levels, not just your to-do list.
    - Why most people suck at time blocking—and how to do it properly.
5. **The Dump Review Offload Plan (DROP) System**
    - The ultimate system for organising your tasks, managing your workload, and making sure things actually get done.
    - How to ditch the never-ending to-do list and focus on what truly moves the needle.
6. **How to Protect Your Time and Set Boundaries That Stick**
    - The truth about time thieves—and how to stop people from stealing your time.
    - How to say "no" without feeling guilty (and without pissing people off).

By the time you finish this book, you'll have a completely new way of managing your time, your workload, and your life.

You'll finally be able to stop feeling overwhelmed, overworked, and constantly behind.

And most importantly, you'll have more time for the things that actually matter.

So, if you're ready to take back control and start making your time work for you, let's get stuck in.

Chapter 2:
The Productivity Myth
Why Working Harder is Holding You Back

Section 1: The Lie We've All Been Sold

The Toxic Productivity Myth

Let's start with a simple question:

Have you ever worked your arse off, long hours, late nights, yet still felt like you were getting nowhere?

You're not alone. Most people believe that working harder is the answer to success. It's what we've been taught since childhood.

For years, we've been fed the same bullshit advice:

"Work harder than everyone else, and you'll get ahead."

"The key to success? Outwork the competition."

"Grind now, rest later."

Sounds inspiring, right? The problem is, it's complete nonsense.

- If hard work alone guaranteed success, then Nurses, teachers, and manual labourers—who work some of the longest hours—would be the highest-paid professionals on the planet.
- The people grinding 70+ hours a week would always outperform those working 40.
- The guy pulling all-nighters at the office would get promoted before the one who leaves at 5 PM.

But that's not how reality works.

Busy vs. Productive: The Key Difference

Most people confuse movement with progress. They equate being busy with being effective. But busyness is an illusion.

Busy people:

- Say yes to everything, filling their schedule with low-impact tasks.
- Work long hours but never seem to get ahead.
- Feel constantly overwhelmed but rarely accomplish big goals.

Productive people:

- Focus on high-impact work that actually moves them forward.
- Say no to things that waste time.
- Get more done in fewer hours because they focus on leverage, not just effort.

The Problem With Hard Work Alone

The hustle culture lie tells you that more effort = more success.

But in reality, effort only matters if it's directed at the right things.

I learned this the hard way.

Years ago, I was running a business, putting in stupidly long hours. My days looked like this:

- Waking up early, skipping breakfast to "get straight to work."
- Juggling dozens of tasks at once—emails, admin, phone calls, client work.
- Burning through 14+ hour days, convinced that I was "grinding my way to success."
- Collapsing into bed at night, exhausted but not actually moving forward.

And do you know what all that grinding got me?

- **Burnout.**
- **Stress.**

- **Zero real progress.**

I wasn't building anything; I was just keeping busy.

The Shift: Working Smarter, Not Harder

The day I finally broke free from the "hard work" trap, I asked myself one question:

"If I had to cut my workday in half, what would I actually focus on?"

That forced me to prioritise what truly mattered instead of just doing more.

The most successful people aren't the ones grinding the hardest.

They're the ones making the smartest decisions.

This doesn't mean hard work isn't important. But if you don't direct it properly, it's just wasted effort.

Key Takeaway: Hard work alone doesn't cut it.
It's about working smarter, focusing on the right things, not just doing more things.

The Difference Between Busy and Productive

The biggest trap we fall into is thinking that if we're working hard, we must be productive.

But let's break it down.

Busy people:

- Fill their schedules with tasks.
- Say "yes" to everything.
- Work long hours but feel constantly behind.
- Confuse movement with progress.

Productive people:

- Focus on high-impact work.
- Say "no" to things that don't matter.

- Get more done in less time.
- Measure success by results, not hours worked.

See the difference?

Busyness feels productive because you're always doing something. But motion without direction is a waste of time.

Here's a perfect example.

Imagine two people in a rowing boat.

- The first-person rows as hard as they can but doesn't check where they're going.
- The second person stops, looks at the map, and then rows in the right direction; even if they row slower, they'll reach the goal faster.

The first person is busy. The second person is productive.

Most people are stuck in constant motion, working hard but not actually moving towards their goals.

The Productivity Trap: Why We Keep Falling for It

So, if hard work doesn't equal success, why do we keep believing the myth?

Because we've been conditioned to think that:

Success = Effort

From school to the workplace, we're rewarded for effort over outcomes:

- At school, we're praised for how much time we spend studying, not whether we've actually learned anything useful.
- At work, we're rewarded for staying late, not for being efficient and getting results faster.
- In life, we admire people who are "always busy" and assume they must be successful.

And social media makes it worse.

Everywhere you look, there's some hustle culture guru telling you:

- "Sleep when you're dead."
- "You have the same 24 hours as Elon Musk; use them better."
- "If you're not working 16-hour days, you don't want success badly enough."

This is absolute nonsense.

Success isn't about grinding more; it's about working smarter.

If it was just about working harder, there'd be no such thing as lazy millionaires, yet we all know they exist.

The real difference between successful people and those who stay stuck?

Successful people focus on impact, not effort.

Breaking Free from the Productivity Myth

If you're constantly working long hours but feel like you're getting nowhere, you don't need to work harder.

You need to work differently.

The first step? Challenge the belief that hard work = success.

Start asking yourself better questions:

- "Am I focusing on high-impact work or just staying busy?"
- "Am I measuring success by hours worked or by results achieved?"
- "If I had to cut my workday in half, what would I prioritise?"

If your answer to any of these is "I don't know", then you're still trapped in the productivity myth, but the good news is, there is still hope; you can break free from it.

In the next section, we'll explore the psychological traps that keep people stuck in overwork and why your brain is wired to sabotage your own productivity (plus how to stop it).

Section 2: The Psychological Traps That Keep You Stuck in Overwork

In the last section, we covered the lie we've been sold, that working harder automatically leads to success. We also explored the difference between being busy and being productive.

But if that's true, why do so many people still fall into the overwork trap?

The answer: your brain is working against you.

There are powerful psychological forces that keep you stuck in the cycle of working harder, even when, deep down, you know it's not getting you anywhere.

In this section, we'll break down the three biggest mental traps that fuel the productivity myth:

- The Effort Justification Trap (Why we equate hard work with success)
- The Addiction to Busyness (Why we crave "feeling productive")
- The Fear of Slowing Down (Why rest feels "lazy" even when it's necessary)

And more importantly, we'll look at how to rewire your thinking so you can escape the cycle for good.

The Effort Justification Trap

(Why We Believe More Effort = More Value)

Imagine you're at a restaurant, and you see two desserts on the menu:

- One is a basic chocolate cake that takes 10 minutes to prepare.
- The other is a hand-crafted, slow-baked soufflé that takes 45 minutes to make.

Which one do you assume is better?

Most people instinctively assume that the soufflé must be superior, not because they've tasted it, but because it requires more effort to make.

This is a psychological bias called effort justification; we tend to overvalue things that require more work, even when they're not actually better.

And it's the same with productivity.

We assume that the person working longer hours must be achieving more, even if their actual results don't back that up.

- The employee who stays late at the office is seen as more dedicated, even if their output is the same as the person who leaves at 5 PM.
- The business owner who works weekends is admired for their "hustle", even if they're just drowning in admin tasks.
- The entrepreneur pulling all-nighters is assumed to be building something great when in reality, they're just terrible at time management.

Here's the uncomfortable truth:

Working long hours feels productive, even when it's not.

Once you fall into the effort justification trap, it's hard to break out of it because your brain wants to believe that all the hard work is necessary.

The Fix:

- Shift from "effort" to "impact" thinking; instead of asking, "How hard am I working?" ask, "What am I actually achieving?"
- Measure success by outcomes, not hours, and track real progress instead of just time spent "being busy."
- Detach your self-worth from your work ethic; working harder doesn't make you "better" or more deserving of success.

The Addiction to Busyness

(Why We Crave "Feeling Productive")

Ever had a day where you ticked off loads of small tasks, answered a ton of emails, and stayed constantly "on the go", but by the end of it, you'd accomplished nothing important?

That's because busyness is addictive.

Your brain releases dopamine (the reward chemical) every time you complete a task, no matter how small. It's the same reason people get addicted to social media notifications; each little "ding" gives your brain a tiny dose of dopamine.

And the more you chase small wins, the more you train your brain to prioritise them over meaningful work.

That's why it's so easy to:

- Spend hours clearing your inbox instead of working on that big project.
- Focus on low-level admin tasks because they're "easy wins."
- Keep checking your phone because it makes you feel busy, even when it's distracting you.

Busyness is comfortable; it gives you the illusion of productivity without the discomfort of tackling harder, more important work.

And before you know it, you're trapped in the cycle of staying busy just to feel like you're being productive.

The Fix:

- Prioritise high-impact work first before getting sucked into low-value tasks.
- Batch low-value tasks together so they don't eat up your whole day.
- Stop confusing motion with progress; just because you're moving doesn't mean you're getting anywhere.

The Fear of Slowing Down

(Why Rest Feels Like Laziness, Even When It's Necessary)

Most people feel guilty when they're not working.

If they take a break, they feel like they're "wasting time." If they finish early, they feel like they should be doing more.

Where does this come from?

It's hardwired into us.

From a young age, we're taught that working harder is morally good and that slowing down is lazy.

- If you're the kid who finishes a school assignment early, you're told to "check your work again" instead of just relaxing.
- If you're an employee who completes your tasks efficiently, you're given more work as a "reward."
- If you run a business and you're not constantly grinding, you feel like you're slacking off.

This creates a deep-rooted fear that if we slow down, we'll fall behind.

And that's why most people never take their foot off the gas, even when they're exhausted, overworked, and running on fumes.

Here's the problem:

Rest isn't the opposite of productivity, it's what makes real productivity possible.

If you're constantly operating at 100%, your brain will eventually hit a wall. You'll start making mistakes, losing focus, and burning out.

Successful people don't work more; they work smarter.

They rest strategically so that when they do work, they perform at their peak.

The Fix:

- Reframe rest as fuel, not laziness; elite athletes don't train 24/7, and neither should you.
- Schedule breaks just like tasks; if you don't plan for recovery, you won't take it.
- Recognise that slowing down isn't falling behind; it's the key to long-term success.

Breaking Free from the Psychological Traps of Overwork

Now that you understand why your brain tricks you into working harder, you can start making better decisions about how you use your time.

Remember:

- Effort doesn't equal value. Working long hours isn't impressive if it's not producing results.
- Busyness isn't productivity. The goal isn't to do more; it's to do what matters.
- Rest isn't laziness. It's what allows you to perform at your highest level.

In the next section, we'll talk about how to shift from the "work harder" mindset to a more effective way of working without sacrificing success.

Section 3: The Shift from Grinding to Working Effectively

In the last section, we exposed the psychological traps that keep people stuck in the overwork cycle, why we equate effort with value, crave busyness, and fear slowing down.

Now, let's talk about how to break free from these patterns.

Because here's the bottom line:

- Success isn't about working harder; it's about working effectively.
- The most productive people aren't the ones grinding the most hours; they're the ones maximising their time and energy.
- If you don't change how you work, you'll keep spinning your wheels no matter how hard you push.

So, in this section, we're going to cover:

- Why effort alone isn't enough, you need leverage.
- The difference between being an operator vs. a strategist.
- How to apply the 80/20 rule to your work.
- How to start doing less, but achieving more.

Let's go.

Effort Alone Isn't Enough, You Need Leverage

Most people think of success like this:

More effort = More results.

This is linear thinking, the idea that if you double your effort, you'll double your output.

But that's not how high performance works.

In reality, success is exponential. The people who achieve massive results aren't the ones grinding harder; they're the ones using leverage to multiply their impact.

What is leverage?

Leverage means getting greater output from the same or less effort.

It's about working smarter, not harder.

Think of it like this:

- A person using a shovel can dig a hole in an hour.
- A person using a bulldozer can dig the same hole in a minute.
- A person who hires someone else to do it doesn't have to dig at all.

The result is the same: the hole gets dug, but the effort required is completely different.

Most people still use a shovel, thinking that "working harder" is the answer, while the most successful people have found the bulldozer.

So, the real question is:

How can you use leverage in your work to achieve bigger results with less effort?

Are You an Operator or a Strategist?

The biggest mistake people make when trying to be productive?

They act like operators instead of strategists.

The Operator Mindset:

- Thinks hard work is the key to success.
- Tries to do everything themselves.
- Spends time on low-impact tasks (emails, admin, busywork).
- Feels stuck in the day-to-day grind.

The Strategist Mindset:

- Focuses on high-leverage work that moves the needle.
- Delegates or automates low-value tasks.
- Spends more time thinking and planning instead of just reacting.
- Knows that efficiency beats effort.

The difference? Operators are always busy. Strategists actually get results.

If you're constantly drowning in small tasks, you're stuck in operator mode.

The shift to being a strategist starts with eliminating, delegating, or automating anything that doesn't truly require you.

And that brings us to one of the most powerful principles of productivity, the 80/20 rule.

The 80/20 Rule: Doing Less, Achieving More

The 80/20 rule (also known as the Pareto Principle) states that:

80% of your results come from 20% of your efforts.

This applies to everything:

- 80% of your revenue comes from 20% of your clients.
- 80% of your productivity comes from 20% of your tasks.
- 80% of your stress comes from 20% of your problems.

But most people spend too much time on the wrong 80%, low-value tasks, minor details, and things that don't actually move the needle.

If you're grinding long hours but not seeing big results, it's likely because you're focused on the wrong work.

Applying the 80/20 Rule to Your Work

To start shifting from overwork to high performance, ask yourself:

What are the 20% of activities that drive 80% of my success?

- These are your high-impact tasks, the ones that directly lead to growth, revenue, or key milestones.

What are the 80% of tasks that take up time but don't actually move me forward?

- These are the things you need to cut, automate, or delegate.

Real-Life Example: How This Works in Business

Let's say you run a business. Here's how the 80/20 rule might apply:

High-value 20% tasks:

- Sales calls that bring in revenue.
- Developing a new product or service.
- Creating content that attracts your ideal clients.

Low-value 80% tasks:

- Checking emails 50 times a day.
- Tweaking your website's font size for the 10th time.
- Attending unnecessary meetings that go nowhere.

Once you identify your 20% of high-impact work, time block it first before anything else fills up your calendar.

The "Less but Better" Approach to Productivity

The highest performers don't just do more; they do less but better.

They're ruthless about where they spend their time.

They:

- Say no to anything that doesn't align with their top priorities.
- Cut out distractions instead of trying to "manage" them.
- Protect their deep work time like their life depends on it.

And this mindset shift alone changes everything.

Most people think productivity is about squeezing in more tasks.

But real productivity is about ruthlessly cutting out anything that isn't essential.

How to Apply "Less But Better" in Your Life

Identify your top 3 priorities each day.

- If you can only accomplish three things today, what are they?
- Block these out in your schedule first.

Stop glorifying busyness.

- Just because you're always working doesn't mean you're doing important work.
- Ask yourself: "If I stopped doing this task, would it actually matter?"

Create "No-Distraction Zones" for deep work.

- Turn off notifications.
- Block out dedicated focus time in your calendar.
- Treat deep work sessions like unbreakable appointments.

Final Thought: The Productivity Mindset Shift

To escape the overwork cycle, you need to rewire your thinking.

You need to go from:

"I need to work harder."
To; "I need to focus on what actually matters."

"Success is about grinding more hours."
To; "Success is about creating more impact in fewer hours."

"If I'm not constantly working, I'm falling behind."
To; "If I work on the right things, I'll get ahead without burning out."

In the next section, we'll get into practical, actionable steps to implement this shift so you can finally break free from the productivity myth and start achieving more while working less.

Section 4: Breaking Free – Practical Steps to Escape the Productivity Myth

At this point, you've seen the truth about the productivity myth, why working harder doesn't guarantee success, why we mistake busyness for progress, and why our brains are wired to keep us in the overwork trap.

Now, it's time to do something about it.

Because knowing this isn't enough. If you don't actively change how you work, you'll keep spinning your wheels, stuck in the same cycle of long hours, stress, and minimal progress.

In this final section, we'll go through:

- How to audit your workload so you know exactly what's driving results vs. what's wasting time.
- The "Stop, Start, Continue" method is a simple framework to shift towards high-impact work.
- How to structure your day for maximum effectiveness without cramming in more tasks.
- The One-Month Challenge is a step-by-step way to break free from the productivity myth for good.

By the time you're done with this, you'll have an actionable plan to finally start working less but achieving more.

Audit Your Workload – What's Actually Moving the Needle?

The first step to escaping the productivity trap is knowing exactly where your time is going.

Most people are unconscious about their work habits. They just react to what's in front of them, assuming that because they're "busy," they must be productive.

But let's test that.

For the next three days, track everything you do in a simple time log. Every hour, jot down:

- What you worked on.
- How long you spent on it.

- Whether it was high-impact or low-impact work.

After three days, review your time log and ask yourself:

- Which tasks actually moved me forward? (Revenue, business growth, progress on key goals.)
- Which tasks were just "filler" work? (Stuff that kept me busy but didn't produce real results.)
- Where did I waste the most time? (Distractions, context switching, pointless meetings.)

This ruthless clarity is essential because once you see how much time is being wasted, you can start cutting the fat from your schedule.

The "Stop, Start, Continue" Method – A Simple Framework for Change

Now that you've audited your workload, it's time to take action.

Use the Stop, Start, Continue method to shift your work habits:

STOP – What's Wasting Time?

Look at your time log; what tasks are draining time without producing results?

Common culprits:

- Checking emails every 10 minutes.
- Attending unnecessary meetings.
- Spending hours on admin that could be automated or outsourced.
- Multitasking and constantly switching between tasks.

Your action: Identify at least three things to stop doing immediately.

START – What Needs More Focus?

What are the high-impact activities you've been neglecting?

Common examples:

- Blocking out distraction-free time for deep work.
- Focusing on revenue-generating activities first.

- Reviewing your work weekly instead of blindly grinding.

Your action: Identify three high-impact habits to start right now.

CONTINUE – What's Already Working?

Not everything needs to change. Some habits are already effective; you just need to do them more consistently.

For example:

- If time blocking is working, refine it.
- If setting boundaries has helped, reinforce them.
- If certain tasks drive big results, double down on them.

Your action: Identify three things to continue doing and commit to reinforcing them.

This simple exercise forces you to take control of your time instead of letting your schedule control you.

Structuring Your Day for Maximum Effectiveness

Now that you've identified what to stop, start, and continue, the next step is designing a daily structure that maximises your impact without overloading your schedule.

The 4-Part High-Impact Workday

Prioritise Deep Work - 2-3 Hours when your concentration levels are at their peak (More on this later)

- Rather than checking emails or taking meetings, dedicate your peak energy hours to high-value work.
- No distractions. No multitasking. Just focused execution.

Batch Admin & Low-Energy Tasks Together (Your less productive slots)

- Instead of checking emails constantly, batch process them 2-3 times a day.
- Group similar tasks (calls, reports, minor admin) together so they don't scatter your focus.

Plan Tomorrow Before You Finish Today

- Spend 10 minutes at the end of each day reviewing what you achieved and scheduling your top 3 priorities for tomorrow.
- This stops you from starting your next day in "reactive mode."

Set Clear Work-Life Boundaries

- Decide in advance when your workday ends, and stick to it.
- Without boundaries, work will expand to fill all available time.

This structure ensures you're doing fewer things better instead of just trying to fit in more.

The One-Month Challenge – Breaking Free from Overwork for Good

Changing your work habits takes consistent action, so here's a one-month challenge to rewire your productivity habits permanently.

Week 1: The Awareness Phase

1. Track your time for 3 days (see Section 1).
2. Identify your biggest timewasters and biggest high-value tasks.
3. Implement Stop, Start, Continue, cut 3 timewasters and commit to 3 high-impact habits.

Week 2: The Deep Work Shift

1. Block out 2-3 hours of deep work each morning before checking emails.
2. Set clear boundaries for your availability (no distractions during deep work).
3. Batch process emails, admin, and low-value tasks in specific time slots.

Week 3: The Efficiency Upgrade

1. Automate or delegate at least one recurring task (reporting, emails, admin).
2. Reduce meeting time by at least 25%, decline unnecessary ones or make them shorter.
3. Use the 80/20 rule to identify your most impactful work.

Week 4: The Long-Term Sustainability Check

1. Review your month; what's worked? What still needs improving?
2. Refine your schedule based on what actually moved the needle.
3. Commit to ongoing weekly reviews to stay on track.

By the end of this one-month experiment, you'll be shocked at how much more you get done in less time.

Final Thought: You Don't Need to Work Harder, You Need to Work Smarter

Let's recap the key takeaways from this chapter:

- Hard work alone doesn't lead to success; strategic work does.
- Being busy is not the same as being productive.
- Your brain is wired to keep you trapped in overwork break the cycle.
- Leverage and efficiency matter more than raw effort.
- Time blocking, deep work, and focus are your biggest weapons.

Most people never escape the productivity myth because they refuse to challenge what they've been taught.

But now? You know better.

In the next chapter, we'll break down the most common productivity myths that keep people stuck and how to replace them with strategies that actually work.

Chapter 3: Flawed Productivity Advice Why Most Productivity Tips Don't Work

Section 1: The Problem with Mainstream Productivity Advice

Why So Much Productivity Advice is Utterly Useless

Let's be honest: most productivity advice is absolute garbage.

Everywhere you look, there's someone preaching the one magic trick that will transform your life:

- "Wake up at 5 AM, and you'll be unstoppable!"
- "Just hustle harder, and success will follow!"
- "Multitasking is the key to getting more done!"
- "If you're not working 16-hour days, you don't want it badly enough!"

You've probably heard some version of these at some point.

And if you've tried them, you've probably felt like a failure when they didn't work for you.

But here's the truth:

Most mainstream productivity advice is written for theoretical humans, not real people with real lives.

It assumes you have:

- Unlimited energy.
- No distractions.
- Full control over your schedule.

But in reality, you have:

- A brain that doesn't function at peak energy 24/7.
- Responsibilities that don't fit neatly into a rigid system.
- A life that is unpredictable and messy.

This is why so many people struggle with productivity; they're trying to follow advice that was never designed for their life, their brain, or their situation.

The Myth of the "One-Size-Fits-All" Productivity System

Most productivity books and gurus push a single "proven" method as if there's one universal solution that works for everyone.

- The 5 AM Club tells you to wake up at the crack of dawn, whether you're a night owl or not.
- Pomodoro Technique tells you to work in 25-minute sprints, even if you thrive in deep work sessions.
- Inbox Zero tells you to clear your emails every day, even if constant email-checking is a massive distraction.

But here's the problem with one-size-fits-all advice:

- It ignores how different people function best.
- It forces you to work against your natural rhythms.
- It creates frustration when you can't stick to a system that doesn't suit you.

Imagine forcing a night owl to wake up at 5 AM because some productivity book said it's the "secret to success."

They'll feel miserable, exhausted, and ineffective, not because they're lazy but because they're fighting their own biology.

This is why productivity should be personal, not just a copy-paste method from someone else's life.

Why Productivity Gurus Get It Wrong

Most productivity "experts" give advice that sounds great in theory but completely falls apart in the real world.

And here's why:

1. They Ignore the Messiness of Real Life

Most productivity methods are designed for people who live in a vacuum, not for people with kids, employees, emails, clients, and constant unexpected chaos.

If you run a business or manage a team, you can't just block out four hours of deep work and ignore everyone. If you have a family, you can't just switch your routine overnight because a book told you to.

Real life is messy. Any productivity system that doesn't account for that is useless.

2. They Assume Willpower is Unlimited

Many productivity systems require insane discipline, as if willpower is an unlimited resource.

But here's the reality:

- Your willpower is finite; it drains throughout the day.
- If a system relies entirely on discipline, it will eventually fail.
- The most effective productivity systems work with your natural energy, not against it.

If you're constantly forcing yourself to follow a system that feels unnatural, you'll eventually burn out and abandon it completely.

3. They Confuse "Hard Work" with Productivity

A lot of mainstream productivity advice is just hustle culture in disguise.

You'll hear things like:

- "If you're not working 100-hour weeks, you don't want it bad enough."
- "The most successful people grind harder than everyone else."
- "You can sleep when you're dead."

This is complete nonsense.

Working harder doesn't automatically make you more productive; overworking yourself usually makes you less effective.

- Long hours = More mistakes.
- Hustle culture = Burnout, not success.
- Overworking = Lower creativity and problem-solving ability.

True productivity isn't about grinding more hours; it's about getting the right things done efficiently.

The Problem with Productivity "Hacks"

Another issue?

Most productivity advice is just a collection of random hacks instead of a real system for getting important work done.

Think about it: how many times have you seen these tips?

- "Use blue light-blocking glasses for better focus."
- "Stand up every 30 minutes to boost energy."
- "Drink more water to stay productive."

These are fine, but they're tiny optimisations, not actual solutions.

If your productivity problems come from:

- Poor time management.
- No clear priorities.
- Constant distractions.

Then, all the hacks in the world won't fix it.

You don't need more tricks; you need a clear, sustainable system that actually works for your life.

What This Means for You

If mainstream productivity advice has never worked for you, it's not your fault.

You're not failing because you're undisciplined or lazy.

You're failing because you've been trying to follow advice that wasn't built for you.

The good news?

You don't have to follow someone else's system; you can build your own.

And in the next sections, we'll cover:

- The most common productivity myths and why they don't work.
- The hidden costs of following bad productivity advice.
- How to build a custom productivity system based on YOUR brain and life.

Real productivity isn't about copying what works for someone else but figuring out what works for you.

Section 2: The Most Common Productivity Myths

In the last section, we looked at how bad productivity advice actively hurts your performance, leading to burnout, frustration, and wasted effort.

Now, let's shift gears.

Because the goal of this book isn't just to call out bad advice; it's to give you a better way forward.

So, in this final section of Chapter 3, we're going to cover:

- How to build a productivity system based on YOUR brain, not someone else's.
- The 3 Key Factors of an Effective Productivity Method.
- How to identify your energy rhythms and work WITH them.
- A simple, step-by-step process to create your own custom system.

And don't worry; everything we introduce here will be explored in greater depth later in the book. You'll get clear, actionable guidance on exactly how to implement each technique, so you don't need to figure it all out right now.

By the end of this section, you'll be able to spot bad productivity advice a mile away and replace it with strategies that actually work.

Myth #1: "Wake Up at 5 AM and You'll Be Successful"

One of the most popular productivity trends in recent years is The 5 AM Club, the idea that waking up ridiculously early is the secret to success.

You've heard it before:

- "Successful people wake up before sunrise!"
- "If you're sleeping in, you're wasting your life!"
- "The early bird gets the worm!"

But here's what they don't tell you:

Waking up at 5 AM is completely useless if you're sleep-deprived and running on fumes.

The truth?

- Your productivity isn't determined by what time you wake up; it's determined by what you do when you're awake.
- Not everyone is wired to be a morning person, and forcing yourself into an unnatural schedule can backfire.
- If you're staying up late and only getting 5 hours of sleep, waking up early will make you LESS productive, not more.

Some of the most successful people in the world are night owls, not early birds. And science backs this up: our chronotype (natural sleep-wake cycle) is largely genetic.

The Fix:

Instead of forcing yourself to wake up early just because some book told you to, focus on aligning your work schedule with your energy levels.

If you're naturally more productive at night? Great, schedule deep work in the evenings.

If you thrive in the morning? Perfect, use that time for high-value work.

The key is to work with your natural rhythms, not against them.

Myth #2: "Hustle Harder and Success Will Follow"

The hustle culture myth tells you that if you just work harder and grind longer, you'll eventually succeed.

- "Sleep is for the weak!"
- "You need to be working 16-hour days if you want to make it!"
- "Outwork everyone else, and you'll win!"

Sounds motivating, right? The problem is, it's complete nonsense.

Here's the reality:

- Overworking doesn't guarantee success.
- More hours don't automatically mean more results.
- Burnout destroys productivity, creativity, and decision-making.

Think about it: If hard work alone determined success, then the hardest-working people (nurses, construction workers, teachers) would be the richest people in the world.

But they're not because hard work without leverage, strategy, and efficiency leads to exhaustion, not success.

The Fix:

- Stop glorifying grinding for the sake of grinding; focus on high-impact work instead.
- Set clear work-life boundaries so you don't burn out.
- Use the 80/20 Rule; focus on the 20% of tasks that drive 80% of your results.

Productivity isn't about doing more; it's about doing the right things efficiently.

Myth #3: "Multitasking Makes You More Efficient"

For years, people have been told that multitasking is the key to productivity.

- "You should be able to juggle multiple things at once."

- "Successful people don't waste time focusing on one thing at a time."
- "If you can't multitask, you're just not efficient enough."

Sounds great, except for one problem:

Multitasking is a productivity killer.

- Your brain can't actually focus on multiple things at once; it just rapidly switches between tasks, burning more mental energy.
- Task-switching reduces efficiency by up to 40% because every time you jump from one thing to another, your brain has to refocus.
- Multitasking leads to more mistakes because your attention is split.

In fact, research shows that people who think they're great multitaskers are actually the worst at it.

The Fix:

- Stop trying to juggle multiple tasks at once; focus on one thing at a time.
- Use time blocking to structure your day and avoid distractions.
- Batch similar tasks together (e.g., emails, calls, admin) instead of switching constantly.

Multitasking feels productive, but in reality, it just slows you down. Single-tasking is the real secret to efficiency.

Myth #4: "Motivation is the Key to Productivity"

How many times have you heard this?

- "You just need to find motivation, and you'll be productive!"
- "Successful people are always motivated!"
- "If you're struggling to get things done, you're just not motivated enough."

This sounds inspiring, but it's completely wrong.

Because here's the truth:

- Motivation is unreliable; it comes and goes.

- If you wait to "feel motivated," you'll never get anything done.
- Successful people don't rely on motivation; they rely on systems, habits, and discipline.

If you only work when you "feel like it," you'll struggle to get anything meaningful done.

The Fix:

- Stop waiting for motivation and build habits that make productivity automatic.
- Use the 5-Minute Rule; commit to just 5 minutes of work (getting started is the hardest part).
- Create a clear system for your work (like time blocking or the Rule of 3) so you don't have to rely on willpower.

Motivation is a bonus, but it's not the foundation of real productivity. Consistency and structure are.

Final Thought: Productivity is About What Works for YOU

If you've been following bad productivity advice and wondering why it's not working, now you know why.

- You don't need to wake up at 5 AM if you're a night owl.
- You don't need to hustle yourself into exhaustion.
- You don't need to juggle 10 things at once.
- You don't need to rely on motivation.

Instead, you need a productivity system that works for YOUR life, YOUR energy levels, and YOUR priorities.

In the next section, we'll look at the hidden costs of following bad productivity advice and why forcing yourself to use the wrong methods can actually make you less productive over time.

Section 3: The Hidden Costs of Following Bad Productivity Advice

In the last section, we dismantled some of the biggest productivity myths, from the lie that waking up at 5 AM makes you successful to the idea that multitasking is a good thing.

But here's the bigger issue:

Following bad productivity advice doesn't just "not work"; it actively makes you worse.

Forcing yourself into systems that don't suit your brain or lifestyle has serious consequences:

- It reduces your actual productivity because you're working against yourself.
- It creates stress and burnout because you're forcing yourself into unrealistic routines.
- It makes you feel like a failure when, in reality, the system was flawed, not you.

In this section, we're going to break down the real damage caused by following the wrong productivity methods and what happens when you fight your natural working style instead of embracing it.

The Productivity Guilt Cycle – When You Feel Like You're Always Behind

One of the biggest problems with bad productivity advice?

It makes you feel like you're the problem when things don't work.

Have you ever tried a new productivity system only to:

- Struggle to keep up with it?
- Fall behind after a few days?
- Feel like you "must not be disciplined enough" to stick with it?

That's not because you're lazy. It's because the system wasn't designed for you in the first place.

How the Productivity Guilt Cycle Works:

1. You read about a new method that promises to make you ultra-productive.
2. You try to implement it, but it doesn't fit your life or energy levels.
3. You fall behind, get frustrated, and blame yourself for not having enough willpower.

4. You feel guilty, assume you're just "not productive enough," and give up.
   5. You look for another new system, repeating the same cycle over and over.

This is why most people never actually become more productive; they're stuck chasing new hacks instead of figuring out what actually works for them.

The Fix:

- Stop assuming you're the problem when a method doesn't work.
- Recognise that productivity is personal; what works for someone else may not work for you.
- Focus on building a system around your strengths rather than forcing yourself into a rigid framework that doesn't fit.

The Burnout Trap – When "Hustle" Leads to Collapse

We live in a world that glorifies overwork.

People brag about how little sleep they get. Social media is full of posts about "grinding" 24/7. Hustle culture tells you that if you're not exhausted, you're not working hard enough.

But let's be real: burnout is NOT a badge of honour.

Studies show that long-term overwork reduces productivity, creativity, and decision-making ability.

Working more than 50 hours per week leads to diminishing returns; beyond that, you're just making more mistakes.

Chronic stress and exhaustion don't make you successful; they make you physically and mentally broken.

And yet, people still push themselves into unsustainable work habits because they think it's the only way to "get ahead."

The Warning Signs of Productivity-Induced Burnout:

- You feel exhausted all the time, even when you sleep enough.
- You struggle to focus, even on simple tasks.

- You feel like you're constantly behind, no matter how much you do.
- You lose motivation for things you used to enjoy.
- Your work quality starts dropping, and you start making more mistakes.

If you recognise any of these, you're already in the burnout zone.

The Fix:

- Stop believing that overworking = success.
- Build work-life boundaries without guilt.
- Focus on efficiency, not just effort, getting the most important things done in less time.

The Problem with Forcing Yourself into the Wrong Routine

Imagine telling a night owl that they need to wake up at 5 AM to be successful.

They drag themselves out of bed, exhausted, and spend the first few hours of the day in a mental fog. By the time they actually feel awake, half their "productive morning" is already wasted.

Now, imagine telling an early bird that they need to work late into the night.

By 8 PM, their brain is done, and they're struggling to focus. But they push on because some productivity book told them to, and their work and health suffer as a result.

This is what happens when you fight your natural energy rhythms instead of working with them.

- Some people thrive in the morning, so they should schedule deep work early.
- Some people hit their stride in the afternoon; they should block out focus time then.
- Some people do their best work at night; forcing them to be "morning people" is counterproductive.

But bad productivity advice ignores these differences and pushes people into routines that actually make them less effective.

The Fix:

- Identify your personal productivity rhythm; when are you naturally most focused?
- Align your deep work blocks with those high-energy periods.
- Stop trying to fit into someone else's schedule; create one that fits you.

(Later in the book, we'll go deeper into chronotypes and why humans evolved with different sleep-wake cycles.)

The Hidden Cost of Constant Context Switching

Most people don't realise how much switching between tasks destroys productivity.

Let's say you're:

- Answering emails.
- Jumping on a call.
- Working on a report.
- Checking social media.

Each time you switch tasks, your brain takes several minutes to refocus.

This means:

Multitasking actually wastes time; you think you're getting more done, but you're just losing around 40% efficiency.

Context switching drains mental energy, leaving you exhausted by midday.

You never enter deep focus mode, which is where real high-value work happens.

The result? You work longer hours but achieve less.

The Fix:

- Batch similar tasks together (e.g., answering emails in one block instead of constantly checking).

- Eliminate unnecessary notifications that pull your attention away.
- Create deep work blocks where you focus on one thing at a time, distraction-free.

Final Thought: Work Smarter, Not Harder

If you've ever felt like no matter how much you work, you're not making progress, this is why:

- Bad productivity advice is holding you back.
- Forcing yourself into the wrong routine will make you LESS productive.
- Hustling harder is NOT the answer; working smarter is.

So what do you do instead?

In the next section, we'll go through how to build a productivity system that actually works for YOU, one that aligns with your natural rhythms, energy levels, and priorities.

Because real productivity isn't about fitting into someone else's method; it's about creating a system that fits you.

Section 4: Try, Test, and Tailor – Finding What Works for You

In the last section, we explored how bad productivity advice does more harm than good, leading to frustration, wasted energy, and burnout. But this book isn't about complaining—it's about action.

This section is your starting point for building a productivity system that works for you, not against you.

We're not jumping into rigid frameworks yet. Instead, we'll explore some key principles and techniques that you can start trialling now. This experimentation will help you build the ultimate system when we dive into the **DROP System** later in the book.

By the end of this section, you'll:

- Understand that productivity isn't one-size-fits-all.
- Learn to embrace trial and error as part of the process.
- Have a toolkit of methods to test and adapt to your own needs.

Why Productivity is Personal (Stop Copying, Start Customising)

Here's the truth: Productivity is as personal as your morning coffee order.

Too many people try to copy someone else's method only to find it doesn't work for them. Maybe you've fallen for:

- The **5 AM Club**: Because apparently, success only comes to those who wake up before the sun.
- The **Pomodoro Technique**: Short, focused sprints that leave you feeling more fragmented than focused.
- **Time Blocking**: A colour-coded calendar that looks great but never survives real-life interruptions.

At first, these systems feel amazing. You're motivated, organised, and on top of everything. But then reality kicks in. You stop following the plan, and suddenly, it's back to chaos.

Why? Because the system wasn't designed for your brain, your lifestyle, or your priorities.

Experimenting with Techniques: A Trial Run for Your Future **DROP System**

You're going to need a system that fits your life like a glove. But finding that system takes time. Start here:

1. Time Blocking

- **What it is:** Dividing your day into blocks dedicated to specific tasks or themes.
- **How to test it:** Instead of planning every hour, start with broad "theme blocks." For example:
    1. Mornings = Deep Work.
    2. Afternoons = Meetings/Admin.
- **What to watch for:** Does this structure help you focus, or does it feel too rigid?

2. The Rule of 3

- **What it is:** Limiting your focus to three high-impact tasks per day.
- **How to test it:** Write down three non-negotiables each morning. If you complete them, the day's a win.
- **What to watch for:** Are you picking tasks that actually move the needle or just the easiest ones?

3. The Pomodoro Technique

- **What it is:** Working in focused sprints (e.g., 25 minutes) with regular breaks.
- **How to test it:** Use it for shallow tasks like emails or admin, and see if it keeps you focused.
- **What to watch for:** Do the sprints feel too short for deep work? If so, extend them to 45 or 60 minutes.

4. Task Batching

- **What it is:** Grouping similar tasks to reduce context switching.
- **How to test it:** Set specific times for emails, calls, or errands instead of scattering them throughout the day.
- **What to watch for:** Does batching make you more efficient, or do interruptions throw you off track?

Your Mission: Test, Tweak, and Track

No system is perfect out of the box. This isn't about getting it right the first time—it's about refining as you go.

Here's your plan:

1. Pick one technique from the list above.
2. Test it for a week. Keep notes on what works and what doesn't.
3. Tweak it until it feels natural. Add flexibility, adjust timeframes, or combine methods.

What's Next?

By trying these methods now, you're laying the groundwork for the **DROP System** later in the book—a framework that ties everything together into a personalised productivity powerhouse.

Remember, this isn't about forcing yourself into a system that feels unnatural. It's about creating one that plays to your strengths, adapts to your energy rhythms, and helps you focus on what truly matters.

Let's get started.

Chapter 4: Finding Your Focus – Time Blocking or The Daily Big Three?

Section 1: The Real Problem isn't Time, It's Focus

Most people who say they "don't have enough time" are lying to themselves.

They don't have a time problem—they have a focus problem.

Because here's the truth: you have all the time you need to get important things done. You just keep filling it with shit that doesn't matter.

And no, I don't mean binge-watching Netflix or scrolling Instagram (though, let's be honest, that probably isn't helping). I'm talking about all the low-value, soul-sucking, time-draining distractions that disguise themselves as work.

Meetings that should have been emails.

Emails that should have been ignored.

Tasks that feel productive but actually achieve nothing.

You've been busy as hell, but at the end of the day, you feel like you've got fuck all to show for it.

That's because you're spending your time reacting instead of focusing.

Busy VS Productive: Most People Don't Know The Difference

A productive person and a busy person can both work 10 hours a day.

The difference?

- The productive person works on high-impact tasks, moves the needle, and makes real progress.
- The busy person spends the day in meetings, answering emails, switching between ten different tasks, and putting out fires—then wonders why they feel exhausted but achieve nothing.

The busy person convinces themselves they're being productive because they're doing a lot of things.

The productive person actually gets important shit done.

One of them controls their time. The other lets everyone else control it for them.

Guess which one most people are?

Why You Always Feel Like You Have No Time

You don't need more time—you need to stop wasting the time you already have.

Every morning, you wake up with 24 hours. Yet, by the time you check your emails, sit through a pointless meeting, and respond to a dozen "urgent" requests, half your day is gone—and you haven't done a single thing that actually moves you forward.

It looks something like this:

- **You start the day with good intentions.** You know what you *should* be doing.
- **You check your emails.** Now, there are ten new things demanding your attention.
- **You open your laptop—Slack is going off.** Someone needs something from you.
- **A meeting gets added to your calendar.** You weren't even asked; it just appeared.
- **Someone "quickly needs your help".** That quick five minutes turns into 30.
- **By midday, you haven't touched a single important task.**
- **At 5 pm, you're exhausted but have nothing to show for it.**

This isn't a lack of time.

This is a failure to protect your time.

If you don't decide in advance what you're going to focus on, the world will decide for you.

And guess what? The world doesn't give a shit about your priorities.

STRUCTURE = FREEDOM

Most people think having a plan will make them feel restricted. That if they schedule their time, they'll lose their flexibility and freedom.

But here's the reality:

Without structure, you have zero freedom.

You're at the mercy of everyone else's requests, priorities, and interruptions.
Your day gets filled with whatever comes at you, not what actually matters.

With structure, you take control.

You decide—before the chaos starts—what's actually worth your time. You get your important shit done first.

And when the distractions inevitably come, you've already won the day.

The question is, how do you build that structure?

That's where **Time Blocking** and **The Daily Big Three** come in.

Some people need strict boundaries and a clear schedule to stay focused.

Others just need a simple way to prioritise what matters most.

That's why this chapter is about two equally effective approaches:

- **Time Blocking** – for people who need structure.
- **The Daily Big Three** – for people who need flexibility.

Neither is better. The best system is the one that works for you.

In the next section, we'll break down Time Blocking, how it works, and how to use it properly (without overcomplicating the hell out of it).

Time Blocking – The Structured Approach

If you're the kind of person who needs clear boundaries, a plan, and a way to shut out distractions, time blocking is for you.

This isn't some overly complex productivity hack—it's just a structured way to make sure you actually do what matters instead of drifting through the day reacting to whatever lands in front of you.

At its core, time blocking is simple:

1. You divide your day into blocks of time.
2. Each block is assigned a task or type of work.
3. When a block starts, you focus on that one thing—nothing else.

That's it.

Instead of leaving your day open-ended and hoping you'll "find time" to work on important things, you decide in advance when those things will happen.

Time blocking forces you to be intentional with your time. It stops you from jumping between tasks, getting distracted, and letting other people's priorities take over your day.

It works because it removes the uncertainty of what to do next. There's no wasted mental energy deciding what to focus on—you've already made that decision ahead of time.

How to Set up Time Blocking Properly

Most people screw up time blocking in one of two ways:

- **They overcomplicate it.** They create a rigid, colour-coded calendar where every minute of the day is planned, leaving no room for real life to happen.
- **They don't actually follow it.** They set up time blocks, but when the time comes, they let distractions creep in or move things around until their plan is meaningless.

The goal here isn't to create the *perfect* plan—it's to create a structure that actually works in the real world.

Here's how to do it properly:

1. **Start with your non-negotiables.** Block out time for anything fixed in your schedule—meetings, calls, deadlines. These are things you **can't** move.
2. **Create blocks for deep work.** If you have tasks that require focus—writing, strategy, problem-solving—set aside **uninterrupted** time for them.
3. **Group similar tasks together.** Instead of spreading admin, emails, or small tasks throughout the day, batch them into dedicated time blocks. This stops you from constantly switching gears.
4. **Leave buffer time.** If your calendar is packed from morning to night, one delay will throw off your entire day. Leave gaps between blocks to absorb the unexpected.
5. **Protect your blocks.** If someone asks for your time during a blocked-out session, treat it like a meeting. You wouldn't cancel a client call just to answer a random email—treat your focus time with the same respect.

Time blocking isn't about controlling every second of your day. It's about making sure the important things get done first, so when the chaos inevitably hits, you're not scrambling to fit them in.

Why Time Blocking Works

The biggest problem most people have with time isn't that they don't have enough of it—it's that they waste too much of it on low-value work, distractions, and pointless interruptions.

Time blocking fixes that by forcing you to:

- **Be intentional.** You're making a conscious decision about how to use your time rather than letting the day dictate itself.
- **Create boundaries.** When you're in a time block, that's all you focus on—no multitasking, no interruptions, no reacting to whatever pops up.
- **Stop drifting.** There's no "what should I do next?" because you've already planned it.

It eliminates decision fatigue. It removes the temptation to jump between tasks. It stops you from reaching 5 pm and wondering where the hell your day went.

When Time Blocking Doesn't Work

Time blocking is one of the most effective ways to take control of your time—but only if you actually stick to it.

It doesn't work if:

- You let people constantly interrupt your schedule.
- You keep pushing things back and reshuffling your blocks.
- You ignore the structure you set and keep jumping between tasks.

And for some people, it just isn't the right system.

If the idea of blocking out your entire day feels restrictive or overwhelming, it might not be the best approach for you. That's fine—there's another option.

In the next section, we'll look at **the daily Big Three**—a flexible approach for those who don't want every hour mapped out but still need a system to stay focused.

Section 3: The 5 Biggest Mistakes People Make with Time Blocking

Time blocking isn't hard, but most people completely screw it up.

They get excited, block out their whole calendar with ambitious plans, and for the first day or two, it feels amazing. They're in control, they're focused, and they're smashing through work like never before.

Then reality kicks in.

By day three, something unexpected happens: a meeting runs over, an urgent email hijacks their morning, or they hit a mental slump in the afternoon. Suddenly, their perfectly planned time blocks start crumbling, and before they know it, they've abandoned the system altogether.

Sound familiar?

If you've ever tried time blocking and found it didn't work, chances are you made one (or more) of these common mistakes.

Let's break them down, and more importantly, let's fix them.

Mistake #1: Treating Time Blocking Like a To-Do List

A to-do list is just a collection of tasks. Time blocking is a structured plan for getting those tasks done. But most people blur the lines between the two.

Here's what happens:

- They take their massive to-do list and dump it straight into their calendar, filling every hour with tasks.
- They feel like they're being productive because everything is scheduled.
- But when the day doesn't go exactly as planned (which it never does), they feel like they've failed.

This is the wrong way to do it.

A to-do list is not a schedule.

The Fix: Separate Planning from Execution

- Step 1: Write out your to-do list first, but don't put everything straight into your calendar.
- Step 2: Identify the high-impact tasks that actually need deep focus. These get dedicated time blocks.
- Step 3: Group smaller tasks (emails, admin, calls) into batch blocks instead of scattering them throughout the day.
- Step 4: Leave buffer time because life will always throw curveballs at you.

A properly time-blocked day isn't just a list of tasks; it's a structured, realistic schedule that allows for flexibility.

Mistake #2: Trying to Plan the "Perfect" Day

If you've ever thought, "Tomorrow, I'm going to have the most productive day ever", and spent an hour crafting the perfect schedule... you've fallen into this trap.

It usually looks something like this:

> 6:00 AM – Wake up, go to the gym, meditate, journal, make a green smoothie
> 8:00 AM – Deep work
> 10:00 AM – Emails
> 11:00 AM – More deep work
> 12:30 PM – Lunch
> 1:00 PM – Client meetings
> 3:00 PM – More deep work
> 5:00 PM – Plan the next day, switch off, enjoy the evening

Sounds fantastic, right? The problem? Real life doesn't work like this.

The moment one thing runs over or an unexpected task pops up, the whole schedule collapses. And instead of adapting, people get frustrated, abandon their plans, and feel like they've failed.

The Fix: Plan for Reality, Not Perfection

The key to making time blocking actually work is building flexibility.

- Use "theme blocks" instead of micromanaging every minute. Instead of scheduling "Write report from 9:00-10:00 AM," just block 9:00-11:00 AM as a Deep Work Block, giving yourself room to adjust.
- Expect the unexpected. Add buffer time between major tasks so that when something overruns, it doesn't derail your whole day.
- Use time blocking as a framework, not a prison. Some days won't go as planned, and that's fine. The goal isn't perfection; it's progress.

Mistake #3: Not Protecting Your Time Blocks

This one's huge.

People time-block their schedule beautifully but then let everyone else hijack it.

Emails pop up, and they stop mid-task to reply.

- Someone calls, and they answer immediately.
- A co-worker or client asks, "Got a minute?" (which is never just a minute).
- Before they know it, the whole day has been dictated by other people's priorities instead of their own.

The Fix: Treat Your Time Blocks Like Important Meetings

- Put your deep work blocks in your calendar like a real appointment. If someone asks for a meeting, you're "already booked."
- Turn off notifications during time blocks. If it's truly urgent, they'll call. If they don't call, it wasn't urgent.
- Batch communication. Instead of checking emails constantly, schedule email processing time and stick to it.
- Communicate your availability. If you have a team, let them know when you're in a focus block and unavailable unless it's an emergency.

You wouldn't answer emails in the middle of a job interview, so why let distractions ruin your focused work? (More on this later in the book)

Mistake #4: Ignoring Your Energy Levels

Most people schedule their work based on time alone.

Big mistake.

Not all hours are created equal. Your energy and focus levels fluctuate throughout the day. Trying to do deep, mentally demanding work when your brain is in "low power mode" is like trying to sprint on an empty stomach; it's a losing battle.

Getting into deep work can feel like a struggle, especially if you're procrastinating. If you find yourself putting things off, sometimes the best way forward is the 5-Minute Rule: just commit to starting for five minutes. More often than not, once you start, you'll keep going. So, use deep work for important, complex tasks, and use quick wins like the 5-Minute Rule to break through resistance when getting started feels impossible.

The Fix: Align Your Schedule with Your Energy Peaks

- Identify when you're naturally most productive. If you do your best work in the morning, schedule deep work for then. If you're a night owl, stop feeling guilty and block off time in the evening.
- Schedule low-energy tasks for low-energy times. Admin, emails, and repetitive work should go in your afternoon slump zones, not in your peak performance hours.
- Test and adjust. Pay attention to when you're most focused vs. when you hit a mental wall. Build your schedule around your natural rhythms.

The best time management strategy isn't about forcing yourself into a rigid system; it's about working with your own biology.

Mistake #5: Thinking Time Blocking is a "One and Done" System

Time blocking is not something you set up once and forget about.

It's a living system, which means it needs regular adjustments. Your priorities shift. Unexpected things come up. A method that worked last month might not work today.

Most people fail at time blocking because they treat it as a rigid, set-in-stone structure.

The Fix: Weekly Reviews & Adjustments

- Every Sunday (or Friday, as I prefer to do), take 10 minutes to review your time blocks. What worked? What didn't? What do you need to tweak?
- Refine your system as you go. If a certain time block keeps failing, adjust it instead of forcing it.
- Time blocking isn't about sticking to a perfect plan; it's about making real progress.

Final Thought: Time Blocking is a Skill, Not a Quick Fix; it is Only Part of The Solution

If time blocking hasn't worked for you in the past, it's not because the system is broken; it's because you weren't using it properly.

The biggest difference between people who succeed with time blocking and those who don't?

The successful ones stick with it, adjust, and make it work for them.

I tried and failed at times, blocking more times than I care to admit in the past. I had the most reactive job; I had too many direct reports needing my time. I had to solve every problem as it arose, but the penny eventually dropped, and I realised the structure of my day was pretty much the same; it was just the specifics that changed. That was the day I made time-blocking work for me.

In the next section, we'll go deeper into advanced time-blocking strategies, including how to balance deep work, meetings, and personal time without feeling overwhelmed.

Section 3: The Daily Big Three – The Flexible Approach

If time blocking feels too rigid, or you hate the idea of planning every hour of your day, there's another way.

It's called The Daily Big Three, and it's as simple as it sounds:

1. Each morning, you choose three high-impact tasks.
2. You work on those three things before anything else.
3. Once they're done, the rest of your day is yours.

Instead of cramming your calendar with scheduled blocks, you just focus on three key things that will make the day a success.

The Daily Big Three works because it forces you to be ruthless about what actually matters. You stop drowning in an endless to-do list and focus on the things that truly move the needle.

Why The Daily Big Three Works

Most people fill their day with low-value tasks that feel productive but don't actually get them anywhere.

- They tick off 15 small things but avoid the one thing that would make a real impact.
- They get to the end of the day exhausted, but when asked what they actually achieved, they struggle to answer.
- They confuse being busy with being productive.

The Daily Big Three forces you to break that cycle.

It's based on a simple rule: If you could only get three things done today, what would they be?

This forces you to:

- **Prioritise what actually matters.** No fluff, no filler—just the work that moves the dial.
- **Cut the noise.** If something doesn't make the Big Three list, it's probably not that important.
- **Create a sense of progress.** At the end of the day, instead of feeling like you ran in circles, you know you tackled the most important things.

It stops you from working on autopilot and forces you to think: *What's actually going to make a difference today?*

How To Make The Daily Big Three Work For You

Just like time blocking, The Daily Big Three only works if you actually commit to it. Here's how to do it properly:

1. **Choose your three tasks the night before.** That way, you start the day knowing exactly what to focus on—no time wasted figuring it out in the morning.
2. **Do them first.** Before checking emails, before scrolling your phone, before getting sucked into other people's problems—start with your Big Three.

3. **Make sure they're actually important.** These aren't just random to-dos. They should be things that **move you forward, solve problems, or create progress**.
4. **Be realistic.** Don't overload your list with massive projects. The Big Three should be **challenging but achievable** within a day.
5. **Don't let other people's priorities hijack your day.** If something urgent comes up, fine—but unless it's a true emergency, your Big Three should still take priority.

If you finish your Big Three early, great—you can move on to smaller tasks. But if all you get done is those three things, the day is still a success.

When The Daily Big Three Doesn't Work

Just like time blocking, The Daily Big Three isn't perfect for everyone. It won't work if:

- **You treat it like a wish list instead of a commitment.** If you pick three tasks but never actually do them, this system is pointless.
- **You don't prioritise high-value work.** If your Big Three is filled with admin tasks that don't actually move you forward, you're just ticking boxes for the sake of it.
- **You constantly let distractions take over.** If your day is dictated by emails and interruptions, you'll never make progress on what actually matters.

For some people, this method alone isn't enough. They need something with more structure.

And that's fine—because just like time blocking, The Daily Big Three isn't a one-size-fits-all solution. It's just one tool.

In the next section, we'll look at how to decide which method is best for you—or how to combine both approaches for maximum impact.

Section 4: The 5 Biggest Mistakes People Make With The Daily Big Three

The Daily Big Three is one of the simplest and most effective productivity systems you can use. But, like anything, most people screw it up.

They either half-arse it, misunderstand it, or turn it into something so bloated and complicated that it stops working.

If you're going to use this system, use it properly. Here are the five biggest mistakes people make—and how to avoid them.

1. Picking The Wrong Tasks

Not everything belongs on your Big Three list.

If you're filling it with random to-dos, low-value admin, or easy wins just to feel productive, you've completely missed the point.

Your Big Three should be the most important thing you can do that day to move forward—not just a dumping ground for whatever tasks happen to be on your mind.

Think about it like this:

- **Good Big Three Tasks:** Writing a proposal that could land a high-value client. Finalising a critical project. Making five sales calls that could lead to new business.
- **Bad Big Three Tasks:** Replying to emails. Filing receipts. Updating your calendar.

The question you should be asking is: If I only get three things done today, what will make the biggest impact?

If your Big Three isn't full of needle-movers, you're just playing at productivity instead of actually getting things done.

2. Letting Other People's Priorities Take Over

Most people start the day in control of their time—and then give it away the moment an email, call, or Slack message comes through.

They set their Big Three, but by midday, their time has been hijacked by urgent but unimportant distractions.

- A colleague needs a quick favour that turns into a 30-minute side task.
- An email pulls them into a problem that wasn't even theirs to deal with.
- A meeting gets scheduled over the time they planned to work on something important.

By the time they look up, the day is nearly over, and their actual priorities have been pushed aside.

Here's the fix:

- Be ruthless. Your Big Three comes first. Everything else waits.
- If something truly urgent comes up, swap it in—but don't just let your list get longer.
- Block time for your Big Three and protect it like you would a meeting. If someone asks for your time, you're "already booked."

Most of the things demanding your attention aren't actually urgent—you're just treating them that way.

3. Making The List And Then Ignoring It

Some people are great at setting their Big Three but terrible at actually doing it.

They make their list in the morning, then get distracted by easier tasks, fall into reactive mode, and completely ignore what they planned.

It's the equivalent of going to the gym, warming up, and then walking straight back out the door.

Your Big Three isn't just a suggestion. It's the contract you make with yourself to get the important shit done.

Here's how to make sure you follow through:

- **Look at your list throughout the day.** If you're "too busy" to even check your Big Three, you're probably wasting time on the wrong things.
- **Do at least one of them first thing.** Before opening emails. Before getting lost in distractions.
- **Don't let yourself finish the day without completing them.** If you have to work a little later to finish, so be it. You made a commitment—keep it.

If you're choosing your Big Three but never actually doing them, you're just making a wish list—not a plan.

4. Choosing Unrealistic Tasks

Your Big Three isn't supposed to be your entire day's work—it's the three highest-impact things you can realistically complete that day.

Too many people get this wrong. They set their Big three as huge, multi-step projects that they have no chance of finishing.

- "Write my entire website."
- "Redesign my business strategy."
- "Sort out my entire financial plan."

These aren't tasks—they're projects.

If something is too big to complete in one sitting, break it down into a task you can actually finish. Instead of *"Write my entire website,"* set *"Write the homepage draft."* Instead of *"Sort out my finances,"* set *"Review last quarter's revenue and expenses."*

The Daily Big Three only works if the tasks are actually finishable. If you keep rolling them over to the next day unfinished, you're doing it wrong.

5. Thinking The Big Three Is All You Have To Do

Some people treat The Daily Big Three like it's the **only** work they have to do.

They pick their three things, finish them by lunchtime, and then waste the rest of the day scrolling social media and feeling like they've done enough.

That's not the point.

The Big Three is your minimum standard—not your maximum output.

It guarantees that even on a bad day, you've done something meaningful. But on a good day, you should still aim to get more done.

Once your Big Three is finished, move on to smaller tasks, follow-ups, or anything else that needs doing. Just don't let the Big Three be an excuse to stop working early unless you genuinely have nothing else important to do.

How To Actually Use The Daily Big Three Properly

If you want this system to work, here's what you need to do:

- Pick high-impact tasks that move you forward. No admin. No fluff.
- Start your day with at least one Big Three task before checking emails or distractions.
- Protect your time. Don't let other people's bullshit push your priorities aside.
- Choose tasks you can actually finish. If something is too big, break it down.
- Don't stop working just because your Big Three is done. Use the rest of your day wisely.

The Daily Big Three isn't about ticking boxes—it's about making real progress on what actually matters.

Section 5: Which One Should You Use?

By now, you've seen two different approaches to structuring your time.

- **Time Blocking** – a structured approach for people who need clear boundaries and dedicated focus time.
- **The Daily Big Three** – a flexible approach for people who need priorities without rigid scheduling.
- **Both** – for some people, using both the daily Big Three and time blocking together proves to be the ultimate productivity system.

Both methods work. Both methods can help you take back control of your time instead of reacting to everyone else's demands.

But which one is right for you?

This section will help you figure that out.

Do You Need Structure Or Flexibility?

The biggest difference between Time Blocking and The Daily Big Three is how much control vs flexibility they offer.

Some people need strict structure to stay focused. If their day isn't planned, they'll drift, procrastinate, or let distractions take over. Time Blocking forces them to stay on track.

Others need more freedom. If they're locked into a rigid schedule, they'll resist it, push tasks around, or feel like they're constantly falling behind. The Daily Big Three gives them focus without feeling trapped.

Here's how to figure out which camp you fall into.

Time Blocking Works Best If…

Time Blocking is the best approach for you if:

- You get easily distracted and need structure to stay on track.
- You thrive on routine and want your day mapped out in advance.
- Your work requires deep focus and long periods of uninterrupted time.
- You struggle with deciding what to do next and waste time switching between tasks.
- You feel like your day is constantly hijacked by other people's demands.

Time Blocking removes decision fatigue because you're not figuring out what to do next—you already decided that in advance.

If you find yourself jumping between tasks, struggling to focus, or spending half the day on reactive work, this method forces you to protect your time and focus on what actually matters.

But Time Blocking isn't perfect.

If your work is unpredictable—if you deal with constant interruptions, last-minute requests, or a schedule that changes frequently—it can feel too rigid. That's where The Daily Big Three might be a better fit.

The Daily Big Three Works Best If...

The Daily Big Three is the better approach if:

- Your schedule is unpredictable, and you can't guarantee fixed time slots.
- You hate the idea of planning your entire day down to the hour.
- You just need a simple way to prioritise what matters without overcomplicating things.
- Your work is task-based rather than time-based.

Instead of boxing your entire day into rigid slots, The Daily Big Three gives you three clear priorities and lets you work on them whenever it makes the most sense.

It works especially well if your work involves a mix of meetings, admin, and project-based tasks that don't always fit neatly into pre-planned time blocks.

But just like Time Blocking, The Daily Big Three isn't perfect.

If you're prone to procrastination, distractions, or letting other people's priorities take over, you might find yourself drifting through the day without making real progress.

That's why some people use both.

Why Some People Combine Both Approaches

The truth is, you don't have to choose one or the other.

Many people find that a combination of Time Blocking and The Daily Big Three gives them the best of both worlds—structure where they need it and flexibility where they don't.

Here's how that works:

1. Time Blocking for Deep Work, The Daily Big Three for Priorities

- Use Time Blocking for focused work that requires dedicated attention.
- Use The Daily Big Three to set the most important tasks of the day.

For example:

- **9:00 AM – 11:00 AM:** Time Block for writing a report.
- **11:00 AM – 11:30 AM:** Emails and admin.
- **11:30 AM – 12:30 PM:** Time Block for a strategy meeting.
- **Afternoon:** Flexible time to tackle the remaining Big Three tasks whenever makes sense.

This way, you get the focus of Time Blocking and the flexibility of The Daily Big Three.

2. Time Blocking for Fixed Tasks, The Daily Big Three for Everything Else

Some tasks need to happen at a specific time: meetings, calls, appointments.

Others just need to get done at some point during the day.

You can use Time Blocking for fixed commitments and The Daily Big Three for everything else.

For example:

- **10:00 AM – 11:00 AM:** Client call (Time Block).
- **2:00 PM – 3:00 PM:** Team meeting (Time Block).
- **Big Three for the day:** Write sales proposal, follow up with a lead, and finalise a project plan.

This gives you structured time where it's needed but still allows flexibility for the rest of your work.

What Happens If You Pick The Wrong System?

Here's the good news: You're not locked into one method forever.

If you try Time Blocking and it feels like too much micromanaging, switch to The Daily Big Three.

If you try The Daily Big Three and find yourself drifting through the day without real focus, switch to Time Blocking.

The only mistake is doing neither and staying stuck in reactive mode, letting distractions control your day.

If you're not sure where to start, pick the system that sounds like it would work best for you—and commit to it for two weeks.

Don't half-arse it. Actually, use it properly.

At the end of the two weeks, ask yourself:

- Am I getting more of the important stuff done?
- Do I feel more in control of my time?
- Am I staying focused, or am I still getting distracted?

If the answer is yes, you've found your system. If not, adjust it, tweak it, or switch methods.

The point isn't to follow one rigid system for the rest of your life—it's to find what actually helps you take back control of your time.

Final Thoughts

Neither of these methods will work unless you actually commit to them.

Time Blocking won't work if you ignore your schedule every time something "urgent" comes up.

The Daily Big Three won't work if you pick random, low-value tasks just to tick them off a list.

Whichever method you choose, use it properly.

Once you do, you'll stop feeling like time is constantly slipping through your fingers. You'll stop reacting all day long and actually make progress on what matters.

No more running in circles. No more working hard and achieving nothing.

Pick a system. Use it. Take back control of your time.

Section 6: Making It Stick – How to Stay Consistent

Deciding which system to use is easy. Sticking with it? That's where most people fall apart.

Because, let's be honest, starting strong is easy. You set up your time blocks, pick your Big Three, feel motivated, and for the first few days, it feels like you've cracked the code.

Then, real life happens.

- You oversleep, miss your first block, and the whole day goes off track.
- A last-minute meeting gets dropped in your calendar, and suddenly, your Big Three is ignored.
- You get distracted, fall back into old habits, and tell yourself you'll "get back on track tomorrow."

One bad day turns into two, and before you know it, you've completely abandoned the system you know works.

This section is about how to stop that from happening **b**ecause knowing what works doesn't mean shit if you don't actually do it consistently**.**

Why Most People Fail at Sticking to a System

Most people don't quit Time Blocking or The Daily Big Three because they "don't work."

They quit because they fall into one of these traps**:**

1. They Expect Perfection

They plan their day down to the minute. They set ambitious Big Three goals. They're convinced this is *the* system that will change everything.

Then, the first thing goes wrong, and they throw the entire plan out the window.

They tell themselves:

- *"I missed my first-time block, so the whole day is ruined."*
- *"I didn't finish my Big Three, so what's the point?"*
- *"I'll just restart fresh on Monday."*

They treat productivity like a diet—one slip-up and they assume they've failed completely.

The truth? There is no perfect day.

Some days will be smooth, and you'll execute everything exactly as planned.
Some days will be chaotic, and you'll barely get through half of what you intended.

Neither of those things means the system is broken. The only way to fail is to quit.

2. They Don't Build It Into a Habit

Anyone can use Time Blocking or The Daily Big Three for a few days when they're feeling motivated.

But motivation is bollocks—it's unreliable.

If you don't turn these systems into a habit, you'll fall off the wagon the moment your motivation dips.

Here's how to make it automatic:

- **Attach it to something you already do.** Pick your Big Three right before you shut down your laptop at the end of the day. Set up your time blocks right after your morning coffee. Tie it to an existing habit so it doesn't get forgotten.

- **Set reminders.** If you forget to check your Big Three by 10 AM, have an alarm that forces you to. If you ignore your time blocks, get a notification reminding you what's next.
- **Do it even when you can't be arsed.** Habits don't care if you "feel like it." The days you least want to do it are the days you need it the most.

3. They Don't Adapt When Things Change

Life isn't static. Some weeks, you'll be slammed with meetings. Some weeks, you'll have more flexibility. If you don't adapt, you'll struggle.

- If your schedule suddenly gets busier, maybe full-time blocking isn't realistic—but keeping a Big Three is.
- If your work is unpredictable, you might need to be more flexible with your time blocks instead of treating them as rigid rules.

The system should fit your life, not the other way around.

4. They Let Distractions Take Over

You can have the best plan in the world, but if you don't protect your time, it's pointless.

Most people fail at consistency because they're too available. They let emails, calls, and last-minute requests dictate their day.

If you let everyone else set your schedule, don't be surprised when your own priorities get ignored.

Here's how to fix that:

- **Say no more often.** Not every request deserves your time.
- **Block distractions during deep work.** Put your phone on silent, close your inbox, and stop letting notifications break your focus.
- **Stick to your plan unless there's a real reason to change it.** Most "urgent" things aren't actually urgent—they just feel that way in the moment.

If you don't take your own time seriously, no one else will either.

How to Stay on Track Long-Term

If you want Time Blocking or The Daily Big Three to actually stick, here's what you need to do:

1. Set a Bare Minimum Standard

Some days, life will get in the way. That's normal. The key is to have a bare minimum level of commitment that you stick to no matter what.

- If you can't do full-time blocking, at least block out one focus session per day.
- If you can't finish your full Big Three, make sure you get at least one priority done.

The goal is progress, not perfection.

2. Do a Weekly Reset

Every week, take 10 minutes to reflect:

- **What worked?** What did I execute well?
- **What didn't work?** Where did I go off track?
- **What will I adjust for next week?**

This keeps you accountable. If you had a bad week, don't just brush it off—figure out what went wrong and adjust.

3. Track Your Wins

Most people quit systems that are working simply because they don't notice the results.

If you've been using Time Blocking or The Daily Big Three consistently, go back and look at how much more you're getting done compared to before.

Even small wins—finishing your work earlier, making faster progress, feeling less overwhelmed—are proof it's working.

Final Thoughts

Time Blocking and The Daily Big Three only work if you actually use them.

They won't magically make you productive just because you like the idea of them.

You have to commit. You have to protect your time. You have to build consistency even when motivation is gone.

If you do that, you'll stop feeling like time is slipping away.

You'll stop ending your days wondering where the hell your hours went.

You'll take back control of your time—and, by extension, your life.

Now it's on you.

Use the system. Stay consistent. Get shit done.

Chapter 5: The Psychology of Procrastination. Why You're Your Own Worst Enemy

Section 1: The Science of Procrastination – Why We Delay What Matters

Let's start with a harsh truth:

Procrastination isn't just about being lazy.

If it were, it would be easy to fix, just "work harder" and "get on with it," right?

But you already know that doesn't work.

Because even when you have:

- A clear deadline.
- A perfectly organised to-do list.
- A genuine desire to get something done…

…you still put it off.

So why do we do this?

The answer lies in how your brain is wired.

In this section, we'll break down:

- The real reason your brain prioritises short-term comfort over long-term success.
- How procrastination is a battle between two parts of your brain.

- Why some tasks feel impossible to start, even when you know they're important.
- The psychological triggers that push you into procrastination mode.

Once you understand what's happening inside your head, you can finally take control and stop letting procrastination run the show.

The Battle in Your Brain – Why You Keep Putting Things Off

When you procrastinate, you're not just making a bad choice; you're actually stuck in a war between two parts of your brain.

1. The Prefrontal Cortex (The Logical Planner) – This is the smart, rational part of your brain. It's responsible for setting goals, making long-term plans, and thinking ahead.
2. The Limbic System (The Instant Gratification Machine) – This is the emotional, survival-focused part of your brain. It's all about avoiding discomfort and seeking pleasure in the moment.

Every time you face a task, especially one that feels hard or uncomfortable, these two parts of your brain start fighting.

- The Prefrontal Cortex says: "This is important. We should start now."
- The Limbic System says: "That sounds stressful. Let's check Instagram instead."

And because the Limbic System is faster and more powerful, it often wins.

End result?

You avoid the task not because you're lazy but because your brain is wired to prioritise short-term comfort over long-term success.

Procrastination is an Emotional Problem, Not a Time Problem

Most people think procrastination is about poor time management, but it's actually an emotional regulation problem.

You don't procrastinate because you "don't have time."

You procrastinate because the task in front of you triggers negative emotions like:

- Stress (It feels overwhelming, so you avoid it.)
- Fear (You worry you'll do it badly, so you don't start.)
- Boredom (It's tedious, so you find something more stimulating.)

Procrastination is your brain's way of saying:

"I don't like how this task makes me feel, so I'm going to avoid it by doing something easier and more enjoyable instead."

This is why:

- You suddenly feel the need to clean your entire house when you have a big deadline coming up.
- You spend an hour scrolling through social media when you know you should be working.
- You convince yourself that you'll "feel more ready" to start tomorrow.

But here's the thing:

The longer you delay, the worse it feels.

Avoiding a task temporarily reduces stress, but in the long run, it makes things worse because the deadline gets closer, and the pressure builds.

The Fix?

You have to learn how to override your brain's default response, which we'll cover later in the chapter.

The Psychological Triggers That Push You into Procrastination Mode

Certain situations increase the chances of procrastination because they trigger stress, fear, or overwhelm.

Let's break down the most common triggers and why they make it so damn hard to start.

Trigger #1: The Task Feels Too Big (Overwhelm Mode)

Have you ever looked at a massive project and thought, "Where the hell do I even start?"

Your brain sees a huge mountain of work and panics. Instead of breaking it down, you shut down completely.

Example: Writing a book feels impossible, so you don't write anything.

Example: Cleaning the entire house feels overwhelming, so you don't clean at all.

Brain Response: "Let's avoid this stress and do something easier."

(Later in the book, we'll cover how to break tasks down using the Rule of 3 and micro-goals.)

Trigger #2: Fear of Failing (Perfectionism Mode)

Sometimes, we procrastinate not because we're lazy but because we're afraid of doing something badly.

Example: You delay sending an important email because you want to "get the wording just right."

Example: You put off launching your business because you're worried it won't be perfect.

Brain Response: "If I don't start, I can't fail."

(We'll go deeper into perfectionism-based procrastination in the next section.)

Trigger #3: The Task is Boring (Instant Gratification Mode)

Your brain craves stimulation. If a task feels tedious, it will look for something more exciting, like checking your phone or watching Netflix.

Example: Studying for an exam is dull, so you keep "taking breaks" every five minutes.

Example: Filing reports is tedious, so you suddenly remember you "need" to reorganise your desk.

Brain Response: "Let's do something fun instead."

(Later, we'll talk about how to use "temptation bundling" to trick your brain into doing boring tasks.)

Trigger #4: No Immediate Consequences (Future Me's Problem Mode)

When a deadline is far away, your brain doesn't see the urgency, so it convinces you that you have plenty of time.

Example: You don't start a project because it's "not due for another two weeks."

Example: You don't save money because "you'll worry about retirement later."

Brain Response: "Future Me can deal with this."

(We'll cover how to create "artificial urgency" to trick your brain into action.)

Why Understanding Procrastination is the First Step to Beating It

Most people try to fight procrastination by forcing themselves to be more disciplined, but that's like trying to stop a speeding car by slamming on the brakes while still pressing the accelerator.

- Discipline alone won't fix procrastination.
- Motivation won't fix it, either.
- Willpower is unreliable; it runs out.

The real fix?

You need to understand what's happening in your brain and use the right strategies to outsmart it.

And that's exactly what we'll cover in the rest of this chapter.

Final Thought: Procrastination is Not a Character Flaw, It's a Psychological Pattern

If you've struggled with procrastination, it's not because you're lazy.

It's because your brain is wired to prioritise short-term comfort over long-term success.

Now that you understand:

- Why procrastination happens.
- How your brain tricks you into avoiding tasks.
- The psychological triggers that push you into procrastination mode.

You can start taking back control.

In the next section, we'll break down the four main types of procrastination, because understanding YOUR specific procrastination style is the key to stopping it.

Section 2: The Four Types of Procrastination – Which One is Wrecking Your Productivity?

Now that we've covered why procrastination happens and how your brain fuels it, let's go deeper.

Because not all procrastination is the same.

Different people procrastinate for different reasons. Some delay work because they fear failure. Others put things off because the task feels too big. Some just get distracted by instant gratification, while others struggle with indecision.

To beat procrastination, you need to know which type you're dealing with.

In this section, we'll break down the four main types of procrastination:

- The Perfectionist – You don't start because you're afraid of doing it "wrong."
- The Overwhelmed Avoider – The task feels too big, so you shut down.
- The Instant Gratification Seeker – You avoid work because distractions feel more fun.
- The Indecisive Overthinker – You spend more time thinking about doing something than actually doing it.

By the end of this section, you'll know exactly which type of procrastination is holding you back and, more importantly, how to stop it.

The Perfectionist Procrastinator – The Fear of Doing It Wrong

- You struggle to start tasks because you're afraid they won't be perfect.
- You spend way too much time "polishing" small details instead of making real progress.
- You'd rather delay a task than risk producing something "average."

If this sounds familiar, you're a perfectionist procrastinator.

The problem?

Perfectionism feels productive, but it's actually just a fancy way of avoiding failure.

Your brain tells you:

- "I can't start this yet; I need to do more research first."
- "I'll just tweak this one little thing… and another… and another."
- "I'll wait until I feel completely ready."

But you'll never feel ready.

And in the meantime? Nothing gets finished.

How to Beat Perfectionist Procrastination

- Use the "80% is good enough" rule – Instead of aiming for perfection, aim for 80% done, then refine later.
- Set a time limit for small tasks – Give yourself a deadline for tweaking details, or you'll never move on.
- Focus on progress, not perfection – Remind yourself that done is better than perfect.

The Overwhelmed Avoider – When the Task Feels Too Big to Start

- You look at a big task and think, "I don't even know where to begin."
- Instead of tackling it, you avoid it completely.

- You end up doing smaller, less important tasks just to feel productive.

If this sounds like you, your main problem is overwhelm.

When your brain sees a huge task, it goes into fight-or-flight mode, and instead of tackling it, you freeze and avoid it.

The result? You waste time on small, easy tasks (emails, admin, pointless "busywork") instead of working on the thing that actually matters.

How to Beat Overwhelmed Procrastination

- Break tasks into tiny steps – Instead of thinking, "I have to write a book," think "I just need to write one paragraph."
- Use the 5-Minute Rule – Commit to working on it for just five minutes. Once you start, it's easier to keep going.
- Start with a "low-effort" entry point – If you don't know where to start, do the easiest part first to build momentum.

(Later in the book, we'll dive deeper into breaking tasks down using micro-goals and the Rule of 3.)

The Instant Gratification Seeker – When Fun Wins Over Work

- You sit down to work... and suddenly feel the urge to check social media.
- You tell yourself "just five minutes" of Netflix, and suddenly an hour is gone.
- You struggle to focus because distractions always seem more appealing than the task at hand.

If this is you, your biggest enemy is dopamine.

Dopamine is the brain's reward chemical; it makes you feel good. And unfortunately, your brain prioritises instant pleasure over long-term rewards.

This is why:

- Scrolling TikTok feels better than starting that difficult project.
- Checking your phone feels more rewarding than writing a report.

- Watching Netflix feels easier than tackling a tough conversation.

It's not that you're lazy; it's that your brain is addicted to quick hits of dopamine.

How to Beat Instant Gratification Procrastination

- Remove the distractions before you start – If your phone is nearby, you'll reach for it. Put it in another room.
- Use Temptation Bundling – Pair a boring task with something enjoyable (e.g., only listen to your favourite podcast while exercising).
- Create a "no choice" environment – If distractions aren't an option, your brain will default to the task at hand.

(Later in the book, we'll cover Focus Hacks to help you train your brain to resist instant gratification.)

The Indecisive Overthinker – When You Can't Make a Decision

- You over-analyse decisions instead of taking action.
- You constantly research and gather information but never move forward.
- You worry about "what ifs" so much that you stay stuck in place.

If this is you, your main issue is decision paralysis.

Your brain tells you:

- "What if I pick the wrong option?"
- "I need more information before I can start."
- "Maybe I should wait and see what happens first."

The problem? Overthinking leads to inaction.

And the longer you delay, the harder the decision becomes.

How to Beat Overthinking Procrastination

- Use the "2-Minute Decision Rule" – If a decision takes less than 2 minutes to make, do it immediately.
- Set a "research limit" – Give yourself a set amount of time to gather information, then commit to making a choice.

- Take imperfect action – Instead of waiting for absolute certainty, make the best decision you can with what you know.

(Later in the book, we'll cover strategies for decision-making and how to move past analysis paralysis.)

Final Thought: Which Type of Procrastinator Are You?

Now that you've seen the four main types of procrastination, which one do you struggle with the most?

- Perfectionist Procrastination – You delay starting because you want it to be perfect.
- Overwhelmed Procrastination – You avoid big tasks because they feel too daunting.
- Instant Gratification Procrastination – You get distracted by quick dopamine hits.
- Overthinking Procrastination – You spend too much time analysing instead of acting.

The good news? Now that you know your specific procrastination style, you can start using the right strategies to beat it.

In the next section, we'll break down how your brain tricks you into procrastinating and the sneaky ways procrastination disguises itself as "productivity."

Section 3: The Procrastination Traps – How Your Brain Tricks You into Doing Nothing

At this point, you know:

- Why procrastination happens (the battle between your rational brain and your emotional brain).
- The four main types of procrastination, and which one is sabotaging you.

But here's the real mind-bender:

Your brain is a master of self-deception.

Procrastination doesn't always look like scrolling TikTok or binge-watching Netflix.

Sometimes, it disguises itself as being productive.

Ever had a day where you felt busy, but at the end of it, you realised you hadn't actually done anything important?

That's procrastination in disguise.

I know this because I've done it. I once had a major report to write, a deadline looming over me. I should have just sat down and started. But instead, I told myself, *"I need to prepare first."*

That "preparation" turned into a full day of watching TED Talks on productivity, reading articles about deep work, and even listening to a podcast on overcoming procrastination. I convinced myself that I was getting into the right mindset, but in reality, I was avoiding the work while tricking myself into thinking I was being productive.

By the end of the day, I felt busy, but when I looked at my report, I had written absolutely nothing. I had let procrastination dress itself up as research. It felt like I was working, but in reality, I was just delaying the hard part, actually doing the work.

This is one of the most dangerous forms of procrastination because it gives you the illusion of progress. You feel like you're doing something valuable, but at the end of the day, you've made no real progress. Recognising this trap is the first step in breaking free from it.

In this section, we'll uncover the sneaky ways your brain tricks you into avoiding meaningful work and what to do about it.

The Productivity Illusion – When "Busy Work" Feels Like Progress

One of the most dangerous procrastination traps?

Looking busy instead of being productive.

Your brain loves feeling like it's making progress, even when it's not.

This is why:

- You clean your desk instead of tackling the actual work.
- You spend an hour organising your to-do list instead of doing anything on it.

- You "research" endlessly but never take action.

It feels productive, but it's just avoidance.

Why This Happens:

Your brain is avoiding discomfort, so instead of working on what actually matters, it finds easier, lower-stakes tasks that give you a false sense of accomplishment.

The Fix:

- Ask yourself: "Is this moving me forward?" – Before doing a task, check if it's actually getting you closer to your goal.
- Use the Rule of 3 – Identify the three most impactful tasks for the day and do them before anything else.
- Beware of "fake work" – If a task is just making you "feel busy" without producing results, ditch it.

(Later in the book, we'll go deeper into how to prioritise work effectively using the Rule of 3.)

The Planning Trap – When You Mistake "Getting Ready" for Getting Things Done

Ever spent hours planning, researching, and preparing but never actually started the work?

That's the planning trap.

Planning feels like progress, but it's just another form of procrastination.

It's sneaky because:

- It feels responsible.
- It feels like you're "getting ready" to take action.
- It's comfortable because it delays actual work.

But at some point, preparation has to stop, and execution has to start.

Why This Happens:

Your brain convinces you that you're not ready yet.

- "I need to do more research before I start."
- "I need to find the perfect time to begin."
- "I'll start once I've planned out every little detail."

But "getting ready" becomes an endless cycle because there's always more you can do.

The Fix:

- Set a Hard Start Date – Instead of waiting until you feel "ready," commit to a fixed date to start.
- Use the 80/20 Rule – Identify the minimum amount of prep needed to start and stop there.
- Take Imperfect Action – Remind yourself that starting messy is better than waiting for perfect conditions.

(Later in the book, we'll talk about the "Minimum Viable First Step" technique to break the planning trap.)

The "One More Thing" Syndrome – When You Delay Work with Fake Deadlines

Ever told yourself, "I'll start right after I finish this one thing", but then another thing pops up, and another, and another?

That's One More Thing Syndrome.

You create fake conditions that have to be met before you can start.

- "I'll start my diet after this weekend."
- "I'll start working on my business once things calm down."
- "I'll write that report after I check my emails."

Except the perfect time never comes.

And before you know it, days, weeks, or even months have passed, and you're still waiting to start.

Why This Happens:

Your brain is creating excuses to delay discomfort by making you believe that you need to complete something else first.

The Fix:

- Call yourself out. – Ask: "Do I actually need to do this first, or am I just stalling?"
- Use a Reverse Deadline. – Instead of waiting for the "perfect time," set a fixed deadline and work backwards from there.
- Take the First Step NOW. – Even if it's small, do something today; there will be no more waiting.

The "I Work Better Under Pressure" Lie – When You Create Unnecessary Stress

Ever waited until the last minute to do something, convincing yourself that you "work better under pressure"?

That's a lie your brain tells you to justify procrastination.

Yes, deadlines force you to focus, but working under pressure also:

- Increases stress.
- Reduces quality.
- Leads to sloppy mistakes.

You don't "work better" under pressure. You just work because you have no other choice.

Why This Happens:

Your brain releases adrenaline under stress, which gives you a short-term focus boost.

But over time, relying on panic mode kills creativity and drains your mental energy.

The Fix:

- Create "Fake Deadlines" – Set personal deadlines before the real ones to avoid last-minute stress.
- Use the 5-Minute Rule – Start tasks early, even if it's just for five minutes.
- Work in Sprints, Not Crashes – Instead of relying on last-minute adrenaline, use short bursts of focused work.

(Later in the book, we'll talk about how to create real urgency without stress using the Parkinson's Law technique.)

Final Thought: Your Brain is Smart, But You're Smarter

- Procrastination isn't just "not doing the work."
- It's the clever ways your brain finds to AVOID the work without you even realising it.
- Being aware of these traps is the first step to escaping them.

Here's what to do now:

1. Think about today: did you fall into any of these procrastination traps?
2. Identify the biggest way your brain tricks you into avoiding work.
3. Use the fixes in this section to start breaking the cycle.

In the next section, we'll cover the most effective, science-backed methods to finally beat procrastination for good.

Section 4: How to Beat Procrastination – A Simple, Science-Backed System That Works

So far, we've covered:

- Why procrastination happens (the battle between logic and emotion in your brain).
- The four main types of procrastination, and how to identify yours.
- The sneaky ways procrastination disguises itself as "productivity."

Now, it's time for the most important part: how to stop procrastinating for good.

Here's the problem:

Most "stop procrastinating" advice is useless.

People say things like:

- "Just be more disciplined."
- "You need more motivation."
- "Just push through it."

But if willpower alone worked, you wouldn't be procrastinating in the first place.

So, instead of vague advice, this section will give you a simple, science-backed system to beat procrastination, which works with your brain instead of against it.

We'll cover:

- The 5-Minute Rule – The easiest way to start anything (even when you don't feel like it).
- The Micro-Goal Method – How to make overwhelming tasks feel effortless.
- The "Burn the Boats" Technique – How to remove escape routes so you have no choice but to act.
- The Follow-Through Habit – How to build long-term discipline (without willpower).

By the end of this section, you'll have a clear, step-by-step method to stop procrastinating and take action immediately.

The 5-Minute Rule – Trick Your Brain Into Starting

The hardest part of any task?

Getting started.

Once you begin, it's usually easier to keep going, but that first step feels impossible.

That's because your brain overestimates how hard a task will be before you start.

The Fix?

The 5-Minute Rule

How It Works:

- Tell yourself you only have to do the task for five minutes.
- If you want to stop after that, you can.
- But once you start, you'll usually keep going.

Don't feel like going to the gym? Just do 5 minutes of stretching.

Dreading writing that report? Just type for 5 minutes.

Avoiding a tough conversation? Just send one message to start it.

Once you start, your brain realises it's not as bad as you thought, and momentum takes over.

Why it works:

- It removes the pressure of "finishing" and just focuses on "starting."
- What happens next: 9 times out of 10, you'll keep going past 5 minutes.
- Even if you stop, you will still make progress, and that's a win.

But this isn't a substitute for deep work—it's a way to get started when you're stuck. Once you've pushed through that resistance, use time blocking to protect long stretches of deep work where the real magic happens.

(Later in the book, we'll cover how to combine this with habit stacking to make it automatic.)

The Micro-Goal Method – Shrinking Big Tasks to Make Them Easy

The #1 cause of procrastination?

The task feels too big, so you shut down.

If your brain sees a task as too overwhelming, it activates your threat response, which is why you freeze, avoid, or find distractions.

The Fix?

Break the task into micro-goals.

How It Works:

- Instead of saying, "I need to write a 10-page report," say, "I just need to write the first sentence."
- Instead of saying, "I need to clean the entire house," say, "I'll just clean this one shelf."
- Instead of saying, "I need to launch a business," say, "I'll just register a domain name today."

Your brain doesn't fear small actions, so once you take the first step, it's easier to keep going.

Why it works:

- Big tasks trigger avoidance; small tasks feel doable.
- What happens next: Micro-goals create momentum, which leads to big results over time.
- Even if you stop, you still chip away at the task, so it's easier to come back to.

(Later in the book, we'll cover the Rule of 3, another way to structure your work without overwhelm.)

The "Burn the Boats" Technique – Remove Your Escape Routes

One reason procrastination thrives?

You always have an easy escape.

- You plan to work, but your phone is right there.
- You want to start a project, but Netflix is calling your name.
- You tell yourself you'll focus, but email notifications keep popping up.

The Fix?

Make procrastination impossible.

This technique comes from an old military strategy: when ancient warriors invaded a new land, they would burn their boats so they couldn't retreat.

The message? No escape. No choice but to move forward.

How to Apply It:

- Make distractions physically impossible. (Put your phone in another room.)
- Publicly commit to a deadline. (Tell someone you'll finish by a certain date; now there's pressure.)
- Create consequences for inaction. (If you don't follow through, you donate money to a cause you hate.)

Why it works:

- When there's no escape, your brain has to focus.
- What happens next: You stop relying on willpower and just take action.
- Even if you mess up, You'll learn from it and take even stronger action next time.

The Follow-Through Habit – How to Build Long-Term Discipline

Let's be brutally honest: starting is one thing. Sticking with it is another.

If you don't follow through, nothing changes.

And this is where most people fail:

- They start strong but lose motivation.
- They take action once but fall back into old habits.
- They wait to "feel inspired" again, but motivation is unreliable.

The Fix?

Turn action into a habit.

How It Works:

- Tie your task to something you already do. (If you already make coffee every morning, use that time to plan your day.)
- Track your progress visually. (Use a habit tracker or cross off a calendar daily; it tricks your brain into wanting to keep the streak.)
- Make it harder to stop than to keep going. (Commit publicly or put money on the line; now quitting has consequences.)

Why it works:

- Habits remove the need for motivation.
- What happens next: Over time, procrastination stops feeling like an option.
- Even if you slip up, Your habit system keeps you on track.

Final Thought: You Don't Need More Motivation, You Need a System

Let's be clear: motivation isn't completely useless. It's just unreliable. When it's there, it can be a great boost. But when it's not, you need habits and systems to keep you moving forward. If you only work when you 'feel like it,' you'll never get consistent results. The solution? Build a system that makes productivity automatic, so even when motivation fails, you still take action.

Try these next time your motivation is nowhere to be found:

- The 5-Minute Rule gets you started.
- The Micro-Goal Method stops overwhelm.
- The "Burn the Boats" Technique removes distractions.
- The Follow-Through Habit builds long-term consistency.

Forget about waiting until you "feel ready."

Take the first step now, even if it's small.

In the next chapter, we'll break down the power of working with, rather than against, our bodies' natural rhythms and why most people still get it completely wrong.

Chapter 6: Understanding Your Own Brain And Natural Productivity Rhythms

Section 1: Deep Work vs. Mundane Tasks – Knowing When to Do What

Most people schedule their day completely wrong, not because they're lazy, but because they don't match the right work to the right energy levels.

They do their hardest, most demanding work when their brain is half-asleep. They waste their best focus hours on emails, meetings, and admin. And they wonder why they're always busy but never making progress.

The truth is, if you don't structure your work around your natural energy peaks and dips, you'll always feel like you're pushing uphill.

This section will cover:

- The difference between deep work and mundane work.
- Why most people are doing the right work at the wrong time.
- How to structure your day so your energy works for you, not against you.

1. The Difference Between Deep Work and Mundane Work

Not all work is created equal.

Some tasks require intense focus, deep thinking, problem-solving, and creativity. Other tasks are repetitive, low-effort, and don't require much mental energy.

Understanding the difference is the key to structuring your day properly.

Deep Work (High-Focus, High-Value Work)

- Writing, planning, or strategic thinking.
- Solving complex problems.
- Learning a new skill or working on high-impact projects.
- Anything that requires undivided attention.

Deep work is where the real progress happens, but only if you protect your time for it.

Mundane Work (Low-Focus, Repetitive Work)

- Checking and responding to emails.
- Scheduling meetings and admin tasks.
- Data entry or filing.
- Any work that can be done while half-distracted.

Mundane work needs to get done, but if you let it take over your best focus hours, it will kill your productivity.

2. Why Most People Do the Right Work at the Wrong Time

Most people don't think about when they do certain tasks; they just react to their inbox, their meetings, and their to-do list.

The problem?

- Emails and admin steal your best focus hours.
- Meetings are scheduled whenever it's 'convenient,' not when it makes sense.
- Deep work gets pushed to the end of the day when your brain is fried.

If you've ever sat down to do focused work only to realise your brain feels like mush, this is why.

Instead of letting random tasks dictate your schedule, you need to start planning around how your energy actually works.

3. How to Structure Your Day for Maximum Productivity

If you want to be more productive without working longer, you need to align your tasks with your natural energy peaks and dips.

Here's how to do it:

Step 1: Identify Your Peak Focus Hours

- When do you feel the sharpest, most focused, and most alert?
- When do you feel like you can dive deep into a task without distractions?
- This is your deep work time; protect it.

Step 2: Schedule Deep Work During Your Best Hours

- Block off 2–3 hours for deep work in your best focus window.
- Treat it like a meeting with yourself, no emails, no distractions.
- Do your hardest, most valuable work at this time.

Step 3: Batch Mundane Work for Low-Energy Times

- Save emails, admin, and easy tasks for when your energy naturally dips.
- These tasks don't require much thinking, so you can get them done even when you're tired.

Step 4: Plan Meetings Strategically

- Meetings are focus killers; don't let them break up your deep work time.
- Where possible, schedule them in the afternoon when your energy is lower.

Step 5: Create a Pre-Work Ritual to Train Your Brain

- Before deep work, do something that signals, "It's time to focus."
- This could be making coffee, putting on headphones, or closing all tabs.
- Over time, this habit triggers your brain into work mode faster.

4. The Real Productivity Hack: Working Smarter, Not Harder

Most people don't need more time; they just need to protect the time they already have.

The difference between high-performers and everyone else?

- They know their peak focus hours and defend them ruthlessly.
- They don't waste their best thinking on emails and admin.
- They work with their brain, not against it.

If you've ever wondered why some people seem to get way more done in less time, this is why.

They aren't working longer. They aren't grinding harder. They're just doing the right work at the right time.

Final Thought: Work With Your Brain, Not Against It

If you keep fighting your own energy levels, you'll always feel like you're struggling to keep up.

Instead, restructure your day to:

- Do deep work when your brain is at its best.
- Save admin and emails for when your energy dips.
- Stop letting distractions steal your most valuable hours.

In the next section, we'll take this a step further by figuring out whether you're a night owl, an early bird, or somewhere in between and how to make that work for you.

Section 2: Night Owl, Early Bird, or In-Between – Identifying Your Chronotype

If you've ever struggled to be productive at a specific time of day, it's not just in your head; it's in your biology.

Some people are wired to wake up early and feel sharp in the morning. Others feel like zombies before 10 AM but come alive at night. And some sit somewhere in between, with a mix of morning and evening energy peaks.

Yet, despite these natural differences, we're constantly told there's a "best" way to structure our day.

- *"Successful people wake up at 5 AM."*
- *"If you want to get ahead, start work before the world wakes up."*
- *"You just need more discipline to be a morning person."*

It's all bollocks.

If you're a night owl, forcing yourself to wake up at 5 AM won't make you more productive; it'll just make you more exhausted.

If you're an early riser, pushing your hardest work too late at night won't unlock some hidden potential. It'll just slow you down.

Instead of fighting your chronotype (your natural biological rhythm), the key to real productivity is understanding it and working with it.

This section will cover:

- What chronotypes are and why they matter.
- How to identify whether you're an early bird, night owl, or in-between.
- How to adjust your schedule to fit your natural rhythm.

What Are Chronotypes & Why Do They Matter?

Your chronotype is your natural biological sleep-wake cycle, controlled by your circadian rhythm. It determines:

- When you feel most awake and alert.
- When your energy naturally dips.
- When you struggle to focus, no matter how much coffee you drink.

Chronotypes aren't just personal preferences; they're genetically programmed.

This means no amount of "just try harder" will permanently turn a night owl into an early riser or vice versa.

The Three Main Chronotypes

Most people fall into one of these three categories:

1. Early Birds (Morning People)

- Feel most alert and focused early in the morning.
- Energy fades in the afternoon.
- Best suited to deep work in the early hours and admin in the afternoon.

2. Night Owls (Evening People)

- Struggle with early mornings but hit peak focus in the evening.
- Feel groggy in the morning, even after a full night's sleep.
- Work best in the afternoon and late at night.

3. In-Betweeners (Somewhere in the Middle)

- Peak alertness mid-morning and early evening.
- Can adapt to either morning or night work but prefer flexibility.
- Need to experiment to find their best deep work hours.

Understanding which one you are means you can plan your day to match when you're naturally at your best.

How to Identify Your Chronotype

If you're not sure which one you are, pay attention to when you feel naturally awake vs. when you struggle.

Here's a simple way to figure it out:

Step 1: Ask Yourself These Questions

- Do you wake up feeling refreshed without an alarm? *(Early bird.)*
- Do you feel like death before 10 AM, no matter how much sleep you get? *(Night owl.)*
- Do you get a second wind of energy in the late afternoon or evening? *(Night owl or in-betweener.)*
- Do you feel most productive mid-morning but crash by 3 PM? *(Early bird or in-betweener.)*
- If you had no schedule, when would you naturally wake up and go to sleep? *(Tells you your most natural rhythm.)*

Step 2: Track Your Energy Levels for a Week

- For the next seven days, note down:
    - When you feel naturally awake and focused.
    - When you hit an energy slump.
    - When you feel most productive.

This will show you your personal energy rhythm, which is far more useful than forcing yourself into someone else's schedule.

How to Work With Your Chronotype (Instead of Fighting It)

Once you know whether you're an early bird, night owl, or in-between, you can start adjusting your schedule to fit your natural rhythm.

For Early Birds

- Schedule deep work early, first thing in the morning, when your brain is sharp.
- Avoid afternoon decision-making; your energy will be lower.
- Wrap up work earlier and get to bed on time to maintain your rhythm.

For Night Owls

- Stop forcing yourself to wake up early; it's working against you.
- Schedule meetings and admin for mornings when you're still warming up.
- Do deep work in the afternoon or evening when your brain is firing properly.

For In-Betweeners

- Identify your two main focus windows, mid-morning and late afternoon.
- Plan deep work during those times and avoid shallow tasks breaking up your best hours.
- Test adjustments and see what works best.

The Key Takeaway: Stop Copying Other People's Schedules

Most productivity advice assumes everyone works the same way.

But here's the reality:

- If you're a night owl, waking up at 5 AM won't magically make you more successful; it'll just make you miserable.
- If you're an early riser, forcing yourself to work late at night won't make you more productive; it'll just slow you down.
- If you're somewhere in between, you need to experiment to find your sweet spot.

Whilst discipline is the key to getting things done, especially those things you really don't want to do, but the real secret to getting more done isn't discipline; it's alignment.

Work with your chronotype, not against it, and you'll get more done without fighting yourself every step of the way.

Final Thought: Find Your Natural Productivity Window & Use It Wisely

Instead of battling your energy levels, start paying attention to:

- When you focus best.
- When you hit an energy slump.
- When you naturally feel motivated to work.

Real productivity isn't about forcing yourself to grind through exhaustion; it's about knowing when you're naturally at your best and protecting those hours for your most important work.

In the next section, we'll take a deeper dive into why humans evolved with different chronotypes and why understanding this history will help you stop feeling guilty about working in a way that actually suits you.

Section 3: The Science Behind Productivity Rhythms (Evolution & Survival Instincts)

Most people think their productivity struggles are a personal failing.

- *"Why can't I focus in the morning like other people?"*
- *"Why do I get a second wind of energy at night when I should be winding down?"*
- *"Why do I crash in the afternoon when there's still loads to do?"*

The reality? It's not your fault. It's biology.

Your productivity rhythms, when you feel alert, when you get tired, and when you focus best, aren't random. They're hardwired into your body from thousands of years of evolution.

Understanding why your brain works the way it does will help you stop fighting your natural energy cycles and start working with them instead of against them.

This section will cover:

- Why humans evolved with different chronotypes.
- How your brain's survival instincts impact productivity.
- Why your mid-afternoon slump isn't laziness, it's biological.

Why Humans Evolved With Different Chronotypes

Imagine a prehistoric tribe.

If everyone in the group woke up and went to sleep at the same time, they'd be sitting ducks for predators. If everyone slept deeply at once, one attack could wipe them all out.

So what happened? Humans evolved with staggered sleep patterns, meaning:

- Some people naturally wake up early and start the day's work.
- Some function better later in the evening, keeping watch while others sleep.
- Others sit somewhere in the middle, adapting based on what the group needs.

This ensured that someone was always awake to protect the tribe.

That's why today, we still have:

- **Early Birds** – The first ones up, ready to start the day.
- **Night Owls** – Naturally alert late at night, keeping watch.
- **In-Betweeners** – Flexible, able to function in both morning and evening.

This isn't some modern "bad habit"; it's a survival instinct that's been passed down for generations.

So, if you're struggling to be a morning person or feeling guilty for not working late, it's because you're fighting thousands of years of evolution.

How Your Brain's Survival Instincts Impact Productivity

Your energy levels throughout the day aren't random, either.

Humans evolved to cycle through alertness and rest periods, ensuring they could stay productive without burning out.

This is why most people naturally experience a rise and fall in energy like this:

- **Morning Boost** – Your body releases cortisol (the wake-up hormone), making you alert.
- **Midday Peak** – A second wave of focus and problem-solving ability.
- **Afternoon Slump** – A natural energy dip (not laziness, just biology).
- **Evening Recharge** – Energy may return in the evening (especially for night owls).

This cycle repeats every single day, whether you acknowledge it or not.

If you're forcing yourself to work against this pattern, trying to push through low-energy periods instead of working around them, you're setting yourself up for failure.

Why Your Mid-Afternoon Slump Isn't Laziness, It's Biological

Ever wondered why you crash around 2–3 PM?

It's not just a sugar crash or a bad night's sleep; it's a built-in survival mechanism.

Back in prehistoric times, early humans would wake up, hunt, gather, and hit a natural lull in the early afternoon.

- The midday heat made movement inefficient.
- Their bodies needed time to digest food.
- A short break meant they had energy left for the rest of the day.

That same biological mechanism still exists today, which is why your energy dips in the afternoon, whether you like it or not.

Most cultures used to work with this rhythm, taking an afternoon break (like the Spanish siesta) before returning to work later.

But modern society ignores this.

- Office jobs demand non-stop productivity from 9 to 5, even when your brain isn't built for it.
- Instead of working around natural energy dips, people drink more coffee and push through, leading to burnout.
- People blame themselves for feeling sluggish when, in reality, it's completely normal.

Instead of fighting this natural lull, smart professionals and business owners structure their work to match their energy cycles.

How to Apply This to Your Work Schedule

Once you understand that your brain follows a biological pattern, you can start structuring your workday to align with it instead of pushing against it.

Step 1: Identify Your Natural Energy Peaks & Dips

- Track your energy levels across the day for a week.
- Look for patterns; when do you feel most focused? When do you slow down?

Step 2: Schedule High-Value Work for Peak Energy Windows

- Do deep work in the morning boost and midday peak.
- Save admin and emails for the afternoon slump.

Step 3: Stop Beating Yourself Up for Energy Dips

- If you struggle to focus in the afternoon, it's not a motivation issue; it's a biological one.
- Instead of forcing work, take a strategic break and recharge.

Step 4: Experiment & Adjust

- Some people recover quickly from the afternoon slump, while others need longer.
- Test different schedules and see what works best for your brain.

Final Thought: You're Not Lazy, You're Wired Differently

If you've ever struggled to focus at certain times of the day, you now know it's not a personal weakness; it's an evolutionary trait.

- Your chronotype determines when you naturally work best.
- Your energy levels follow a biological rhythm, not a to-do list.
- Your afternoon slump is a survival mechanism, not a sign of laziness.

Instead of fighting your body, start working with it and watch your productivity skyrocket.

In the next section, we'll explore why forcing yourself into an unnatural routine backfires and how to avoid productivity burnout.

Section 4: Why Forcing Yourself Into an Unnatural Routine Backfires

Modern productivity culture is obsessed with **forcing routines onto people**, regardless of whether they actually work for them.

- *"Wake up at 5 AM if you want to be successful."*
- *"Grind harder and stop making excuses."*
- *"If you can't focus, you just need more discipline."*

All of this is complete rubbish.

Yes, discipline matters. But forcing yourself into a routine that goes against your natural productivity rhythm isn't discipline; it's sabotage.

If you're an evening person trying to be productive at 5 AM, you're setting yourself up to fail.

If you're an early riser forcing yourself to push through late-night work, you're tanking your efficiency.

Instead of blindly following someone else's routine, you need to design one that actually works for you.

This section will cover:

- Why forcing yourself into the wrong schedule destroys productivity.
- Why your brain resists unnatural routines.
- How to create a productivity routine that fits your natural rhythm.

Why Forcing the Wrong Schedule Destroys Productivity

When people try to follow rigid productivity routines that don't suit them, two things happen:

1. **They burn out.**
   - Forcing yourself to be productive when your brain isn't wired for it is exhausting.
   - You're fighting your biology instead of leveraging it.
2. **They feel like failures.**
   - If you struggle with a routine that "works for everyone else," you assume you're the problem.
   - You start thinking you need more motivation, more discipline, more caffeine.

But the problem isn't you; it's the system you're trying to use.

Forcing yourself into an unnatural routine is like driving a car with the handbrake on; you can push harder, but you'll never reach top speed.

Why Your Brain Resists Unnatural Routines

Your brain loves consistency, but only if it matches how you're wired.

When you try to force an unnatural schedule, you're working against:

- **Your circadian rhythm** – The biological clock that controls when you feel alert vs. when you get tired.
- **Your energy cycles** – The natural highs and lows that determine when you're most productive.
- **Your cognitive load** – The mental effort required to override your instincts and force yourself into a different schedule.

The result?

- More mental fatigue.
- Less motivation.
- A constant feeling of being drained, even if you're "doing everything right."

Instead of blaming yourself for not fitting into a one-size-fits-all productivity system, you need to build a system that works for your brain, your energy, and your life.

How to Create a Productivity Routine That Works for You

Step 1: Identify Your Natural Work Rhythms

- When do you feel most alert? *(That's your deep work window.)*
- When do you feel your energy drop? *(That's when you should schedule low-effort tasks.)*
- When do you naturally wake up and go to sleep if you don't set an alarm? *(This tells you your ideal schedule.)*

Step 2: Build a Routine That Aligns With Your Energy

- If you're an early bird, schedule deep work in the morning.
- If you're a night owl, schedule deep work later in the day.
- If you're in between, experiment to find your best productivity window.

Step 3: Make Small Adjustments (Not Extreme Changes)

- If your routine isn't working, tweak it gradually; don't overhaul your entire schedule overnight.
- Shift your deep work sessions by 30-minute increments until you find what feels right.

Step 4: Ignore Productivity Gurus Who Sell a Single System

- Productivity is not about copying someone else's schedule; it's about optimising your own.
- If a method feels unnatural, draining, or difficult to maintain, it's probably not right for you.

The Harsh Truth About Productivity Systems

Most people don't need a new productivity hack; they just need to stop forcing themselves into broken systems.

So:

STOP: Trying to wake up at 5 AM when you're wired for late nights…
START: Schedule deep work when you actually feel awake and alert.

STOP: Pushing through brain fog in the afternoon slump…
START: Shift important work to your peak hours and save admin for low-energy times.

STOP: Feeling guilty for not working like someone else…
START: Design a routine that works for you, not against you.

Because the truth is:

- No single routine works for everyone.
- Your brain will always win against a schedule that doesn't suit it.
- Real productivity happens when you work in sync with your biology, not against it.

Final Thought: Productivity Should Feel Natural, Not Forced

If your current routine feels like a constant struggle, you don't need more willpower; you need a better approach.

- Stop fighting your energy levels.
- Stop feeling guilty for not following someone else's routine.
- Start building a schedule that actually fits how your brain works.

When you do that, productivity stops feeling like a battle and starts feeling easy.

In the next section, we'll tackle one of the biggest lies in productivity culture, why "The 5 AM Club" is complete nonsense, and why one-size-fits-all routines don't work.

Section 5: The Myth of *The 5 AM Club* – Why One-Size-Fits-All Routines Don't Work

If you've ever read a productivity book, you've probably seen some version of this claim:

- *"The most successful people wake up at 5 AM."*
- *"If you're serious about getting ahead, you'll start your day before the world wakes up."*
- *"Success starts with the right morning routine."*

It sounds inspiring. Motivational. Like some secret formula that will suddenly make you more productive than ever.

There's just one problem, it's complete bollocks.

Waking up at 5 AM isn't inherently productive.

If you're naturally wired to wake up early, sure, it works. But if you're forcing yourself into an unnatural routine, you're just robbing yourself of sleep, energy, and effectiveness.

The reality? It's not about when you wake up; it's about what you do with the hours you're awake.

This section will cover:

- Where the 5 AM myth came from.
- Why forcing early mornings can backfire.
- What actually matters more than your wake-up time?

Where Did the 5 AM Myth Come From?

The idea that waking up early equals success has been pushed by productivity gurus for years.

It's based on the idea that many successful people wake up early, including:

- CEOs
- Athletes
- Entrepreneurs

But here's what they don't tell you:

1. These people don't wake up early because it makes them successful; they do it because it fits their natural rhythm.
2. For every successful early riser, there's an equally successful night owl.

The reason waking up early works for some people is that they're naturally wired that way.

But for night owls? It's a disaster.

Why Forcing Early Mornings Can Backfire

If you're naturally an early riser, waking up at 5 AM might be great.

If you're not, here's what happens when you force it:

- You sacrifice sleep – Most people don't shift their bedtime early enough, so they just end up exhausted.
- Your brain isn't firing properly – If you wake up before your body is ready, your cognitive function suffers.
- Your productivity tanks – Instead of being effective, you spend your mornings feeling groggy and useless.

The biggest lie about waking up at 5 AM is that it gives you extra time.

It doesn't.

You still have the same 24 hours; you're just shifting them around. And if you're cutting into sleep and making yourself tired before your natural peak productivity times, you're actually making yourself less productive, not more.

What Actually Matters More Than Your Wake-Up Time?

Instead of obsessing over what time you wake up, focus on how you use your best energy hours.

Step 1: Figure Out When You Work Best

- If you feel most focused in the morning, use that time for deep work.

- If you peak in the afternoon or evening, structure your workday around that.
- Stop forcing yourself to be productive at times that don't suit you.

Step 2: Prioritise Sleep Over Stupid Productivity Trends

- Sleep isn't a waste of time; it's what makes you more effective.
- Cutting sleep in favour of waking up early is counterproductive.
- Aim for quality sleep and structure your routine around that.

Step 3: Build a Routine That Works for YOU

- Some people work best with a solid morning routine; others don't.
- Some people thrive on early starts, others do better later in the day.
- The key is alignment, not trying to copy someone else's schedule.

The Bottom Line: Work Smarter, Not Earlier

If waking up at 5 AM fits your natural rhythm, great. Do it.

But if it doesn't?

- Stop forcing yourself to do it.
- Stop feeling guilty because some productivity guru said you should.
- Stop believing success is dictated by an alarm clock.

Because the truth is:

- There is no universal "best" time to wake up.
- What matters is when you work best, not when you get out of bed.
- If you force yourself into a routine that doesn't fit, you'll always be working at a disadvantage.

Success isn't about waking up early; it's about using your best hours effectively.

In the next section, we'll go even deeper, looking at how to work with your biological clock to maximise your productivity without burning out.

Section 6: How to Work With, Not Against, Your Biological Clock

By now, you know that forcing yourself into a routine that doesn't suit you is a losing battle.

You can either:

1. Keep fighting your natural energy patterns, burning out and getting nowhere.
2. Work with your biological clock, aligning your schedule to when you're naturally at your best.

Most people are stuck in option one, blindly following productivity advice that ignores how their brain actually functions.

If you want to work smarter (not harder), you need to understand your biological clock and structure your day around it.

This section will cover:

- How your internal clock affects productivity.
- How to optimise your work schedule for peak efficiency.
- How to avoid common mistakes people make when trying to force productivity.

What is Your Biological Clock & Why Does it Matter?

Your biological clock (aka circadian rhythm) controls your:

- Energy levels throughout the day.
- Focus and cognitive function.
- Sleep-wake cycle.

It's not something you can turn off or override; it's hardwired into your body.

Your circadian rhythm follows a natural pattern of highs and lows, and these dictate your best and worst times for deep work.

Ignoring it = exhaustion, low focus, and wasted effort.

Working with it = effortless productivity and better results.

How to Optimise Your Work Schedule for Peak Efficiency

The key to maximising productivity isn't working longer hours; it's working at the right times.

Here's how to structure your day based on your biological clock:

Step 1: Identify Your Energy Peaks & Dips

Everyone has natural high-energy and low-energy windows throughout the day.

- **Peak focus times** = Best for deep, creative, high-value work.
- **Low-energy times** = Best for admin, shallow tasks, and breaks.

Track your energy levels for a week to find your personal pattern.

Step 2: Schedule Deep Work During High-Energy Hours

- If you're an **early bird**, do deep work first thing in the morning.
- If you're a **night owl**, schedule deep work in the afternoon or evening.
- If you're **somewhere in between**, use your mid-morning and late-afternoon focus peaks.

This is where you do the hardest, most important work: problem-solving, strategy, planning, and creative tasks.

Step 3: Save Low-Energy Times for Admin & Easy Work

Your afternoon slump isn't the time to push through deep work. It's when your brain is crying out for a break.

Use low-energy times for:

- Emails and admin.
- Calls and meetings.
- Planning, organising, or reviewing tasks.

Step 4: Use Breaks to Boost Productivity (Not Kill It)

Instead of mindlessly scrolling your phone, take intentional breaks that actually refresh your brain.

Try:

- A 5–10 minute walk to reset your focus.
- A short meditation or breathing exercise to reduce mental fatigue.
- Listening to music or stepping away from screens to give your brain a reset.

This helps you recharge faster, so when you return to work, you're actually ready to focus.

The Biggest Mistakes People Make When Trying to Be More Productive

Even when people start working **with their biological clock**, they often fall into these traps:

Mistake 1: Forcing Productivity When Energy is Low

- Trying to push through deep work in the afternoon slump = disaster.
- If your brain isn't firing, accept it and shift your tasks accordingly.

Mistake 2: Ignoring Sleep & Expecting to Function at 100%

- Sleep isn't optional; it's fuel for your brain.
- If you're tired, your focus, memory, and problem-solving ability all take a massive hit.

Mistake 3: Failing to Protect Peak Focus Hours

- Don't waste your best energy on emails, pointless meetings, or admin.
- Block out your deep work time and defend it like your business depends on it because it does.

The Ultimate Productivity Hack: Alignment, Not Force

When you stop forcing productivity and start aligning your schedule with your natural rhythms, everything gets easier.

You'll:

- Get more done in less time.
- Feel less exhausted at the end of the day.
- Finally work in a way that feels effortless, not like a battle.

The real secret to productivity isn't waking up earlier, working longer, or grinding harder; it's working smarter by leveraging your brain's natural strengths.

In the next section, we'll cover how to track your energy levels for a week so you can start structuring your schedule based on real data, not guesswork.

Section 7: Action Step – Track Your Energy Levels for a Week & Adjust Your Schedule

Now that you understand how your biological clock affects productivity, it's time to put this knowledge into action.

You can't optimise your work schedule if you don't know when you function at your best.

This final section is a practical exercise, a simple but powerful method to track your energy levels over the next week and start adjusting your schedule accordingly.

By the end of this, you'll:

- Know exactly when you're naturally most focused and when you dip.
- Identify your best deep work windows and your ideal times for admin.
- Stop wasting energy fighting against your biological rhythm.

Let's get started.

Step 1: Track Your Energy Levels for a Week

For the next seven days, you're going to log your energy and focus levels at different points throughout the day.

You don't need to overcomplicate it; a simple rating system will do.

How to Track Your Energy & Focus

At **four key times each day**, rate your:

- **Energy level** (1 = exhausted, 5 = fully alert).
- **Focus level** (1 = distracted, 5 = deep concentration).

Suggested times to check in:

- Morning (1–2 hours after waking up).
- Midday (before lunch).
- Afternoon (midway through your workday).
- Evening (after dinner but before bed).

You can write this down in a notebook, log it in a spreadsheet, or even use a simple notes app on your phone.

Step 2: Identify Your Patterns

After a few days, you'll start noticing clear trends.

Look for:

Your Peak Focus Windows – When do you naturally feel the most alert and productive?

Your Energy Dips – When do you struggle the most?

Your Second Wind – Do you get an energy boost later in the day?

Most people will see obvious trends, for example:

- **Early birds**: Peak in the morning, fade by mid-afternoon.
- **Night owls**: Struggle in the morning and peak in the evening.
- **In-betweeners**: Have two focus windows, late morning and late afternoon.

Step 3: Adjust Your Schedule Based on Your Data

Once you've tracked your energy for a week, it's time to start making adjustments.

Here's how:

If you're a morning person:

- Schedule deep work first thing in the morning when your brain is sharp.
- Block off the first 2–3 hours of your day for focused tasks.
- Save admin, calls, and meetings for the afternoon when your energy dips.

If you're a night owl:

- Stop forcing yourself to do deep work early in the morning.
- Handle low-effort tasks first and ease into your workday.
- Block off your peak afternoon/evening hours for deep work.

If you're in between:

- Use your mid-morning focus peak for your most important work.
- Take a proper break in the afternoon to recharge before your second focus window.
- Schedule low-energy tasks when you naturally dip.

This isn't about overhauling your life overnight; it's about making small but meaningful changes that help you work more effectively without burning yourself out.

Step 4: Refine & Experiment Until You Get It Right

Your first attempt won't be perfect, and that's fine.

After adjusting your schedule, keep tracking for another week and ask yourself:

- Am I getting more done in less time?
- Do I feel less exhausted at the end of the day?
- Is my schedule easier to stick to?

If something still doesn't feel right, tweak it.

This process is about testing, refining, and finding what works for you, not forcing yourself into a rigid system that doesn't fit.

Final Thought: Your Schedule Should Work for You, Not Against You

If you've spent years fighting your natural energy levels, this is your chance to finally work in sync with them instead.

By tracking and adjusting, you'll:

- Work when your brain is at its best.
- Stop wasting your peak energy on useless tasks.
- Feel more productive without working longer hours.

Real productivity isn't about working harder; it's about working at the right times.

This marks the end of Chapter 6, setting you up for the next step: applying these insights to build a bulletproof productivity system that actually works for you.

Chapter 7: Brain Dumping Clearing Mental Clutter to Get More Done

Section 1: Why Your Brain is a Terrible Place to Store Tasks

Your brain is brilliant, but it's also one of the worst places to store tasks, ideas, and reminders.

Yet most people treat their brain like a filing cabinet, stuffing it with:

- Tasks they need to complete.
- Ideas they don't want to forget.
- Random thoughts that pop up throughout the day.
- Commitments, deadlines, and things they "should" do.

Then, they wonder why they feel overwhelmed, stressed, and constantly behind.

The problem?

Your brain isn't designed to store information long-term, it's designed to process, problem-solve, and focus on the present.

The more mental clutter you hold onto, the less focus, energy, and creativity you have for the things that actually matter.

This section will cover:

- Why your brain is terrible at remembering things.
- The science behind mental overload and why it kills productivity.
- Why trying to "keep everything in your head" leads to stress, procrastination, and burnout.

Your Brain is a Thinking Machine, Not a Storage Unit

If you've ever thought, *"I'll remember that later,"* only to completely forget about it, you've already seen how unreliable your brain is at holding onto tasks.

That's because your brain is built for problem-solving, not storage.

Neurologically speaking, your brain has two main types of memory:

1. Short-Term Memory (Working Memory)

- Can only hold a few things at once (typically 4–7 bits of information).
- Quickly forgets things unless they're written down or repeated.

2. Long-Term Memory

- Stores things like skills, knowledge, and experiences over time.
- Hard to access quickly, so it is not ideal for daily tasks and reminders.

The issue? Most people try to store tasks in short-term memory, which isn't built for long-term storage.

This is why you forget things at the worst possible moment; your brain is constantly dumping old information to make room for new data.

Why Mental Overload Kills Productivity

When your brain is holding onto too many loose tasks, three things happen:

1. You feel constantly overwhelmed.
    - A cluttered mind leads to stress, anxiety, and decision fatigue.
    - You struggle to focus because you're juggling too much at once.
2. You waste mental energy remembering things instead of doing them.
    - Your brain keeps looping through unfinished tasks (this is called the Zeigarnik Effect).

- Instead of focusing on what you're doing, you're mentally bouncing between what you need to remember.
3. You forget things at the worst possible time.
    - Important tasks slip through the cracks.
    - You suddenly remember things in the middle of the night (or when you're nowhere near your work).

Sound familiar?

This is why you feel drained by the end of the day, even when you haven't completed much.

Your brain is working twice as hard trying to remember things instead of just doing them.

The Dangerous Myth of "I'll Remember That Later"

Most people don't write things down because they trust themselves to remember.

But here's the truth:

Your brain isn't built for long-term task management.

- If something isn't written down, there's a good chance it will be forgotten.
- If you're relying on memory alone, you're setting yourself up to drop the ball.
- If you're constantly holding onto mental clutter, you're slowing yourself down.

This is why highly productive people don't rely on memory; they rely on systems.

The First Step to Mental Clarity: Stop Using Your Brain as a Task Manager

If you want to be more productive, the first step is getting everything out of your head and into a trusted system.

This is where Brain Dumping comes in, a powerful technique that:

- Clears mental clutter.
- Reduces stress and mental fatigue.
- Frees up focus for deep, meaningful work.

Instead of letting your brain struggle to hold onto tasks, you need a system that ensures:

- Nothing gets forgotten.
- You always know what needs to be done.
- You can focus on execution, not remembering.

This is what we'll cover in the next section: How a Brain Dump Creates Clarity and Reduces Overwhelm.

Section 2: How a Brain Dump Creates Clarity and Reduces Overwhelm

If you've ever felt like your brain is a messy desk cluttered with thoughts, half-remembered tasks, and things you *know* you should be doing, you need a brain dump.

A brain dump is the ultimate mental decluttering technique. It's a simple but powerful process that gets everything out of your head and into a system you can trust.

The result?

- **Instant mental clarity.**
- **Reduced stress and anxiety.**
- **More focus and less procrastination.**

This section will cover:

- Why a brain dump is the fastest way to clear mental clutter.
- How it reduces stress and mental fatigue.
- Why you'll get more done once everything is out of your head.

Why a Brain Dump is the Fastest Way to Clear Mental Clutter

Most people carry their entire to-do list in their heads.

This means they're constantly:

- Juggling unfinished tasks while trying to focus.
- Forgetting things, then remembering them at the worst time.
- Feeling overwhelmed because there's no clear plan.

A brain dump solves this in minutes.

What is a Brain Dump?

A brain dump is exactly what it sounds like: you take every single task, idea, and commitment floating around in your head and get it onto paper or a digital note.

- It's not about organising yet; it's just about getting everything out.
- It's like taking the trash out of your brain so you can finally think clearly.

Once your mind is free of mental clutter, you can actually start making decisions and getting things done.

How a Brain Dump Reduces Stress and Mental Fatigue

Your brain is constantly trying to remind you of unfinished tasks.

This is called the **Zeigarnik Effect**, a psychological phenomenon where your brain fixates on incomplete tasks until they're resolved.

This is why:

- You suddenly remember things at 2 AM.
- Your to-do list feels endless, even if you're getting things done.
- You struggle to focus because your brain keeps jumping between tasks.

A brain dump breaks this cycle.

By writing everything down, you're telling your brain:

- *"I've captured this; there's no need to keep reminding me."*
- *"It's safe in a system. I won't forget it."*
- *"Now I can focus without distraction."*

The result?

- Mental clarity.
- Less stress.
- More focus for deep work.

My First Brain Dump: The Moment It All Clicked

For years, my brain was a 24/7 to-do list.

I'd go to bed feeling wired, running through everything I needed to remember. Then, like clockwork, I'd wake up at 2 AM with an 'Oh Shit' moment, realising I'd forgotten something important.

So, I'd grab my phone, email myself a reminder, and try to go back to sleep.

But my brain wouldn't shut up. I'd toss and turn, worrying about what else I might have forgotten. By morning, I'd already be playing catch-up before the day had even started.

Then, one night, I tried something different. I did a full brain dump.

- I grabbed a notebook and wrote everything down: work tasks, life admin, random thoughts, and things I'd been meaning to do for weeks.
- I didn't organise it; I just emptied my head onto the page.
- Then, I sorted everything into where it actually needed to go: my task manager, my calendar, and my notes.

And that night? I slept like a baby.

No more 2 AM panic. No more emailing myself reminders in the dark. My brain finally trusted that everything was written down in the place I'd action it so it could switch off.

Since that day, I've never gone to bed with loose thoughts floating around in my head. And I've never woken up panicking that I've forgotten something.

Why You'll Get More Done Once Everything is Out of Your Head

Once you've dumped everything onto paper, you can finally:

1. **See the full picture.**
    - No more half-remembered tasks.

- No more "Oh shit, I forgot about that" moments.
2. **Make decisions with clarity.**
    - You can prioritise what actually matters.
    - You can stop wasting time on unimportant tasks.
3. **Stop feeling overwhelmed.**
    - When everything is floating around in your head, it feels like too much to handle.
    - Once it's on paper, you can break it down into clear steps.

This is why brain dumping is the first step to real productivity.

If you don't get tasks out of your head, you'll always be mentally juggling, which leads to stress, procrastination, and wasted time.

The First Step to Productivity is Emptying Your Mind

The difference between productive people and those who are constantly overwhelmed?

Productive people don't trust their memory; they trust their system.

- They don't rely on mental storage.
- They don't spend their day trying to remember things.
- They don't feel mentally exhausted from juggling tasks.

Instead, they capture everything, clear their mind, and focus on execution.

In the next section, we'll go deeper into how to structure your brain dump so that tasks don't just sit on a list; they get done.

Section 3: Building the System – Sorting Brain Dump Tasks into Delete, Delegate, or Do

A **brain dump on its own isn't enough**.

If you stop at simply writing everything down, all you've done is create a long, unfiltered list of stress. You'll still look at it and think:

- *"Where the hell do I start?"*
- *"This list is overwhelming."*
- *"I don't have time to do all this."*

The secret to making a brain dump actually work is sorting everything into three simple categories:

1. Delete – Tasks that aren't worth your time.

2. Delegate – Tasks that shouldn't be done by you.

3. Do – Tasks that require your focus and action.

This quick decision-making process clears out the bullshit and ensures you're only spending time on what truly matters.

Why Most People Struggle After a Brain Dump

A brain dump on its own doesn't solve the problem; it just shows you how much is in your head.

The mistake most people make is treating every single task as something that must be done.

Reality check: It doesn't.

Not everything on your list is important. Not everything needs to be done by you. And some things? They should be deleted altogether.

This is where the **Delete, Delegate, Do** method comes in.

Step 1: Delete – Cut the Crap & Reduce Your Workload

Most to-do lists are full of rubbish, things that feel urgent but don't actually matter.

Before you do anything else, go through your brain dump and ruthlessly delete anything that:

- Isn't important anymore.
- Won't move the needle in your life or business.
- Is there out of obligation rather than necessity.

Ask yourself:

- *"If I never did this, would it actually matter?"*
- *"Is this just busy work disguised as productivity?"*

- *"Am I keeping this task just because it feels comfo.*

Rule: If it doesn't add value, **delete it.**

The fewer unnecessary tasks you keep, the more mental b. .width you free up for real work.

Step 2: Delegate – Get It Off Your Plate

Next, identify the tasks that need to get done but NOT by you.

This includes:

- Repetitive admin tasks.
- Things that someone else on your team can handle.
- Work that would be better outsourced to an expert.

Too many people hold onto tasks they should be passing off, either because they don't trust others to do them, or they believe *"it's quicker if I just do it myself."*

Rule: If someone else can do it **80% as well as you**, **delegate it.**

Your job isn't to do everything; it's to focus on the highest-value work that actually moves the needle.

Step 3: Do – Focus on What Actually Matters

Once you've deleted the unnecessary and delegated what you shouldn't be doing, the only tasks left are the ones that actually need your time and attention.

This is your real to-do list, the work that requires your focus, energy, and decision-making.

How to Prioritise What to Do First

Now that your list is streamlined ask yourself:

1. **What's urgent?** (Deadlines, time-sensitive tasks.)
2. **What's high-impact?** (Tasks that will move the needle.)
3. **What's deep work?** (Tasks requiring serious focus.)

..ule: Schedule **your highest-impact tasks first**, then batch everything else efficiently.

The Power of the Delete, Delegate, Do Method

When you apply this simple three-step process, your overwhelming brain dump transforms into a clear, actionable plan.

- Tasks that don't matter? Gone.
- Tasks that aren't your responsibility? Handled.
- Tasks that need your attention? Organised and prioritised.

No more staring at an endless list, feeling paralysed. No more wasting time on pointless tasks.

Just clarity, control, and a focused plan of action.

Making This a Daily Habit

A brain dump isn't a one-time fix; it's a habit.

To keep your workload under control, follow this system every day or week:

1. Brain dump everything on your mind.
2. Sort tasks immediately into Delete, Delegate, or Do.
3. Take action; don't let the list sit there.

The more you filter your tasks through this system, the more effortless it becomes.

In the next section, we'll go even further, showing you how to build the Capture Habit so you never let mental clutter pile up again.

Section 4: The Capture Habit – Writing Everything Down Immediately

Most people don't struggle with doing tasks; they struggle with keeping track of what actually needs to be done.

It's not that you don't want to be productive. It's that:

- You forget important tasks until it's too late.

- You remember things at the worst possible moment (like 2 AM or mid-shower).
- You're constantly mentally juggling your to-do list instead of executing it.

The solution? The Capture Habit.

The Capture Habit is the practice of immediately writing down every task, idea, or commitment the moment it enters your mind before your brain can forget it.

This section will cover:

- Why your brain can't be trusted to remember things.
- How capturing tasks immediately frees up mental space.
- The best tools and methods for capturing information.

Your Brain is Built to Forget Things (and That's a Problem)

You know that moment when you suddenly remember something important, then five minutes later… it's gone?

That's because your brain isn't designed for long-term task storage, it's designed for problem-solving.

The scientific reality is that:

- Your short-term memory can only hold 4–7 pieces of information at once.
- If a thought isn't written down or repeated, your brain dumps it to make room for new information.
- This is why you forget random tasks until they suddenly hit you later.

Relying on memory to manage your tasks is like writing them on a whiteboard in the rain; sooner or later, they'll disappear.

The Capture Habit: How Writing Things Down Instantly Boosts Productivity

The fastest way to reduce mental stress is to capture everything the moment it enters your mind.

- A task pops into your head? Write it down.
- You remember something while driving? Use voice notes.
- A client asks for something? Add it to your task manager immediately.

This stops your brain from wasting energy trying to hold onto things because now, everything is stored in a trusted system.

The result?

- You never forget tasks again.
- You stop feeling mentally overloaded.
- Your brain is free to focus on real work, not remembering stuff.

Where to Capture Information (and How to Avoid the 'Scrap Paper Trap')

Notebooks, apps, sticky notes, where should you capture everything?

Here's the golden rule: Wherever you write things down, there must be a place you actually check later.

Otherwise, you'll just create a collection of forgotten notes.

Best Tools for Capturing Tasks & Ideas

- **Digital Notes** (Evernote, Notion, Apple Notes, Google Keep) – Great for capturing random ideas on the go.
- **Task Managers** (Google Task, Todoist, ClickUp, Asana, Trello) – Best for capturing work-related tasks immediately.
- **Paper Notebook** – My favourite because it never goes out of date! Ideal if you process notes daily (but avoid Post-it notes scattered everywhere).
- **Voice Notes** – Great for quick task capturing when you're driving or on the move.

Rule: It doesn't matter where you capture tasks as long as you always check and process them later.

The Key to Long-Term Success: Reviewing & Processing Your Captured Tasks

Capturing tasks is only half the battle; the real power comes from actually reviewing and processing them.

How to Build the Habit:

1. Capture tasks immediately, don't trust your brain to remember them.
2. Set a time daily (or weekly) to review and organise your captured notes.
3. Use the Delete, Delegate, Do method to quickly process them.

The more automated this habit becomes, the less mental stress you'll carry every day.

Final Thought: Free Your Brain, Free Your Time

The difference between overwhelmed people and productive people isn't effort; it's how they manage information.

Unproductive people hold everything in their heads, constantly stressing about what they might forget.

Productive people capture tasks immediately, store them in a system, and never waste energy worrying about what they've forgotten.

Your brain isn't meant to be a task list; it's meant to solve problems, make decisions, and create solutions.

So stop trusting your memory. Start trusting your system. And watch your productivity skyrocket.

In the next section, we'll cover where to store tasks so they actually get done instead of being forgotten in a notebook or task manager.

Section 5: Where to Store Tasks So They Actually Get Done

Capturing tasks is only half the battle; the real challenge is storing them somewhere they won't be forgotten.

Most people dump tasks into random places, notebooks, emails, and sticky notes, then wonder why things still slip through the cracks.

The truth is, if your tasks aren't stored in the right place, they may as well not exist.

This section will cover:

- The difference between capturing and storing tasks.
- The three types of task storage every productive person needs.
- How to stop tasks from getting lost in the chaos.

The Difference Between Capturing and Storing Tasks

Writing things down doesn't guarantee they'll get done.

Most people's mistakes? They capture tasks but never organise them.

- They scribble notes in a random notebook and forget about them.
- They send reminders to themselves but never check their inbox.
- They dump everything into a task manager but never schedule anything.

Rule: Capturing is step one. Storing tasks somewhere you'll actually take action is step two.

If you don't have a clear system for storing and reviewing tasks, your brain will still try to hold onto everything, which defeats the entire point of a brain dump.

The Three Types of Task Storage Every Productive Person Needs

To make sure nothing gets forgotten, you need three key storage areas:

1. A Primary Task Manager (For All Actionable Tasks)

This is where every task that needs doing goes, with no exceptions.

Best tools:

- **Todoist** – Simple, fast, and easy for daily task management.
- **ClickUp/Asana/Trello** – Great for managing multiple projects.
- **Apple Reminders/Google Tasks** – Best for personal to-dos or to integrate into your calendar.

Rule: If a task isn't in your primary task manager, **it doesn't exist.**

2. A Calendar (For Anything Time-Sensitive)

Not all tasks need a calendar entry, but anything with a deadline or time requirement does.

Best tools:

- **Google Calendar / Apple Calendar / Outlook Calendar** – For scheduling work tasks and commitments.
- **Time-blocking apps** – If you want to allocate specific time slots to tasks. (Calendar apps can work just as well for this if you use them properly)

Rule: If it has a deadline or needs a specific time to be completed, it belongs in your calendar.

3. A Notes System (For Ideas, Long-Term Plans & Reference Material)

Not every brain dump task is actionable right now; some things are ideas, long-term projects, or just useful info.

Best tools:

- **Notion / Evernote** – For storing research, ideas, and meeting notes.
- **Apple Notes / Google Keep** – For quick idea capture.
- **The Good Old-fashioned Paper Notebook** – If you prefer writing by hand (but review it regularly).

Rule: If it's not an immediate task, store it in a dedicated notes system so you can revisit it later.

How to Stop Tasks From Getting Lost in the Chaos

To make this system work effortlessly, follow these three simple habits:

1. Process Your Brain Dump Daily or Weekly

- Set 5–10 minutes to review your brain dump and sort tasks into the right storage system.
- If a task takes less than 2 minutes, do it immediately.
- Everything else? **Schedule it, delegate it, or delete it.**

2. Keep Your System Clean & Simple

- One task manager, one calendar, one notes system.
- If you store things in too many places, you won't check them.
- Delete irrelevant tasks and notes regularly.

3. Stick to One Golden Rule: Always Trust Your System

- If a task isn't in your task manager or calendar, assume it doesn't exist.
- Don't second-guess whether you "might" remember something, write it down, store it properly, and move on.

Final Thought: Build a System You Can Rely On

A brain dump only works if you know exactly where tasks are going and how they'll get done.

- Capture everything immediately.
- Store tasks where they belong.
- Review and process them regularly.

If you get this right, you'll never stress about forgetting something again.

In the next section, we'll take this even further with an action step to do a full brain dump and structure your next week around it.

Section 6: Action Step – Do a Full Brain Dump Structure Your Next Week Around It

You've now got everything you need to master the process.

- You know why your brain is a terrible place to store tasks.
- You understand how a brain dump reduces stress and mental overload.
- You've got a clear system for sorting tasks into Delete, Delegate, or Do.
- You've built the Capture Habit, so nothing slips through the cracks.
- You know where to store tasks, so they actually get done.

Now, it's time to put it into action.

This section will walk you through doing a full brain dump and structuring your next week around it.

Step One: Do a Full Brain Dump

Set aside 10–15 minutes to empty your brain onto paper (or into a digital note).

Write down everything that's currently floating around in your head:

- **Work tasks** – Deadlines, projects, follow-ups, admin work.
- **Personal tasks** – Errands, appointments, things you've been meaning to do.
- **Recurring tasks** – Weekly/monthly responsibilities you don't want to forget.
- **Big ideas & goals** – Long-term projects, future plans.
- **Random thoughts** – Anything else taking up mental space.

Don't filter. Don't organise. Just dump everything.

Step Two: Sort Using Delete, Delegate, Do

Now, go through your brain dump line by line and categorise each task:

- **DELETE** – Cross out anything that isn't important or necessary.
- **DELEGATE** – Assign tasks that don't require you to do them.
- **DO** – These are tasks that require your time and attention.

Your massive list is now smaller, clearer, and more manageable.

Step Three: Schedule What Matters

Take your **DO** list and structure your next week using:

- **Your Calendar** – Time-sensitive tasks and appointments.
- **Your Task Manager** – Everything that needs doing but doesn't require a fixed time.
- **Your Notes System** – Anything that isn't urgent but needs to be saved.

Rule: If a task isn't in your calendar or task manager, **it doesn't exist.**

Step Four: Make Brain Dumping a Habit

A brain dump is not a one-time fix; it's a weekly and daily habit that keeps you in control.

How to make it stick:

1. End every workday with a quick brain dump.
2. Do a full weekly brain dump on Sunday or Monday to plan the week ahead.
3. Trust your system; if it's written down and scheduled, you can let it go.

The more consistent you are, the less mental clutter you'll have to deal with.

Final Thought: Control Your Brain, Control Your Life

Mastering this system means:

- You'll never feel mentally overloaded again.
- You'll always know what needs to be done and when.
- You'll stop waking up at 2 AM panicking about forgotten tasks.

Your brain is for thinking, not storing information.

So, use it for what it does best: solving problems, making decisions, and getting things done.

Now that you've got everything out of your head and into a system, you're ready for the next step: Time blocking, turning your structured list into a powerful daily plan.

Chapter 8: The DROP System

Section 1: The DROP System – Why You Need Your Own Framework

Let's get one thing straight from the start: This isn't another rigid, one-size-fits-all productivity system.

You know the type, those methods that claim to be "the ultimate way to work," only for you to try them and realise they don't fit your energy levels, responsibilities, or brain chemistry.

The DROP System isn't about forcing yourself into a predefined box. It's about taking control of your time, working with your natural rhythms, and building a system that actually fits your life.

Now, originally, I wanted to call this the **Get Shit Done System** because, let's be honest, that's what most of us are trying to do. But after speaking to people who apparently know better than me, I decided to tone it down a bit so as not to deter the squares of the world. So here we are, The DROP System.

This chapter is about pulling everything we've covered so far together so you can create a tailored productivity system that works for you, not just for the guy who wakes up at 5 AM, drinks green smoothies, and swears by a bullet journal.

The Problem with Generic Productivity Systems

If you've ever tried a well-known productivity system, be it the Pomodoro Technique, GTD (Getting Things Done), or the 5 AM Club approach, and found yourself struggling to stick with it, it's not because you're lazy or undisciplined.

It's because most of these systems weren't designed for you in the first place.

Why Most Productivity Advice Fails

It assumes everyone's brain works the same way.

- Not everyone thrives on early mornings.
- Not everyone focuses best in 25-minute sprints.
- Not everyone needs a perfectly organised to-do list.

It doesn't consider your natural productivity rhythms.

- A night owl forcing themselves into a 5 AM routine is a recipe for disaster.
- A parent juggling work and family life can't always follow strict schedules.
- Some people need structure; others need flexibility.

It ignores the real challenge: execution.

- Fancy productivity hacks are useless if you can't stick with them.
- A system needs to be practical, simple, and repeatable, not overly complicated.

The **DROP System** fixes all of this.

Why The DROP System Works for Everyone (Without Being One-Size-Fits-All)

Instead of forcing a single method on you, the DROP System is about picking the tools and strategies that actually work for you and ditching the rest.

It's built around three core principles:

- **Simplicity** – The less friction, the better. If a system is too complicated, you won't use it.
- **Flexibility** – It adjusts to your energy levels, work style, and real-life commitments.
- **Execution Over Perfection** – The best system is the one you'll actually follow. Done is better than perfect.

What You'll Build in This Chapter

In this chapter, we'll put all the pieces together so you can create your personalised productivity system.

You'll learn how to:

- **Use Brain Dumping** to clear your head and prioritise tasks.
- **Apply the Delete, Delegate, Do Method** to instantly reduce your workload.
- **Work with your natural productivity rhythms** to schedule tasks at the right times.
- **Capture tasks properly** so nothing slips through the cracks.
- **Structure your time with Time Blocking** (or an alternative method that works for you).
- **Refine and tweak your system** so it evolves with your needs.

By the end of this, you'll have a real working system that fits your life rather than a productivity method that demands you change who you are.

Real productivity isn't about squeezing more into your day; it's about making the time you have work better for you.

In the next section, we'll break down the core elements of the DROP System, the foundation you'll use to create your own personalised workflow.

Section 2: The Core Elements of the DROP System

Now that we've established that one-size-fits-all productivity systems are bullshit, it's time to build something that actually works on your terms.

The DROP System = Dump, Review, Offload, Plan.

- **Dump** (Get everything out of your head)
- **Review** (Assess what truly matters)
- **Offload** (Remove, automate or delegate unnecessary tasks)
- **Plan** (Organise and schedule what remains)

The **DROP System** is based on three core principles:

- **Simplicity** – If it's complicated, you won't stick to it.
- **Flexibility** – It adapts to your energy levels, work style, and commitments.
- **Execution Over Perfection** – A half-done task is better than a perfectly planned one that never happens.

These principles ensure that whatever system you build, it's realistic, sustainable, and actually makes your life easier.

1. Simplicity: Productivity Shouldn't Feel Like a Second Job

Most people overcomplicate productivity.

They spend more time organising tasks than actually doing them.

Ever found yourself:

- Colour-coding tasks in a fancy app instead of finishing them?
- Spending hours setting up the perfect Notion workspace?
- Feeling like you need a degree in time management just to plan your week?

That's not productivity, that's procrastination.

The DROP Approach:

- Keep your system lean and efficient with no overcomplicated workflows.
- Use the fewest tools necessary; every extra step is an opportunity to fall off track.
- Stick to simple, repeatable habits, not productivity theatre.

Your system should make your life easier, not harder.

2. Flexibility: Productivity Needs to Work With You, Not Against You

Most rigid productivity systems fail because they don't adapt to real life.

- Some days, you're firing on all cylinders; other days, you're dragging yourself through the mud.
- Sometimes, your plan works perfectly; sometimes, life throws a spanner in it.
- Some people work best in structured blocks; others need more fluidity.

The DROP Approach:

- Design your system around your natural energy levels (not some guru's ideal routine).
- Allow for controlled chaos; leave room for unpredictability.
- Learn to adjust on the fly because no plan survives first contact with reality.

The goal isn't to follow a system perfectly; it's to have a system that works even when things don't go according to plan.

3. Execution Over Perfection: Stop Planning, Start Doing

Some people get so caught up in productivity hacks that they forget the point of getting things done.

The perfect planner won't help you if you never take action.

- Waiting for the "right time" to start? That's procrastination.
- Tweaking your to-do list endlessly? That's resistance disguised as planning.
- Thinking you need to "perfect" your system before using it? That's an excuse.

The **DROP** Approach:

- Prioritise execution over organisation; done is better than perfect.
- Focus on quick wins; momentum creates motivation.
- Develop the habit of starting, even when you don't feel ready.

We talked in Chapter 5 about how motivation is unreliable, and that's true—you can't build success by waiting to 'feel like it.' But does that mean motivation is useless? Not at all. The key is to create conditions that make action easier so that motivation naturally follows. Ever notice how getting started is the hardest part, but once you're in motion, it's easier to keep going? That's why small wins matter. Use momentum—not motivation—to carry you forward. Build habits and systems first, and motivation will show up as a byproduct, not the driver.

The DROP System in Action

Bringing these three principles together, here's what the **DROP System** looks like in practice:

- **A simple workflow** that doesn't require constant tweaking.
- **A flexible approach** that adapts to your energy and schedule.
- **A bias for action**, you do the work instead of over-planning it.

This isn't about creating another rigid system; it's about designing a personalised, high-impact workflow that works for you, not against you.

In the next section, we'll build your personal productivity system using all the tools from the book so you can take control of your time and work on your terms.

Section 3: Assembling Your Personal Productivity System

Now, it's time to put all the pieces together.

This is where you take everything you've learned so far and build a productivity system that actually fits your life.

- No rigid rules.
- No forcing yourself into a system that doesn't work for you.
- Just **a** simple, flexible, high-impact workflow that helps you take control of your time without burning out.

Step One: Choose Your Core Tools

You don't need a million apps, a colour-coded planner, or a bullet journal with gold-trimmed pages.

You need three things:

1. **A Capture System** – To brain dump everything so nothing slips through the cracks.
2. **A Task Management System** – To keep track of what needs doing and when.
3. **A Calendar or Scheduling Method** – To block out time for focused work.

Example Setups

Minimalist Approach:

- Apple Notes for capturing tasks.
- A simple to-do list (Todoist, Google Tasks, or pen & paper).
- Google Calendar for scheduling deep work.

Structured Approach:

- Notion/Evernote for capturing & organising information.
- ClickUp/Trello for task management.
- Time blocking in Google Calendar.

Chaos-Tolerant Approach:

- Voice memos & quick notes for capturing ideas.
- A running list in a simple notes app.
- Flexible, non-rigid time blocking.

Hybrid Approach: (Most people will land somewhere between these.)

- Capture tasks in a way that suits you.
- Store them in a to-do list or task manager.
- Schedule deep work but allow room for flexibility.

Rule: Your system should be **as simple as possible, but no simpler.**

Step Two: Implement the Delete, Delegate, Do System

Once you've captured your tasks, you need to filter them fast; otherwise, your list will become a dumping ground instead of an action plan.

That's where **Delete, Delegate, Do** comes in.

Every time you process your list, ask yourself:

Can I DELETE this?

- If it's not important, cross it off.
- Stop doing tasks just because you've always done them.

Can I DELEGATE this?

- If it doesn't require you, pass it off.
- Handoff admin work, repetitive tasks, or anything someone else can do.

Do I NEED to DO this myself?

- If it's high-impact or requires your expertise, schedule it and get it done.

Rule: If a task doesn't fall into one of these three categories, it shouldn't be on your list.

Step Three: Work With Your Productivity Rhythms

Your productivity system is only effective if you schedule tasks at the right time.

- Are you an early bird? Block deep work in the morning.
- Are you a night owl? Do creative work when you naturally focus best.
- Do you have erratic energy levels? Plan around your high-focus windows and avoid deep work when you're drained.

Rule: Work **with your brain**, not against it.

Step Four: Structure Your Day for Maximum Output

Now that you know what needs doing and when you work best, it's time to structure your day.

In Chapter 4, we covered time blocking—a great tool if you like structured schedules. But what if rigid time slots don't work for you? That's where the Daily Big Three comes in. Instead of blocking out every hour, you focus on knocking out the three most important tasks of the day. However, they fit into your schedule. Neither approach is 'better'; it's about what keeps you on track without overwhelming you. Some people thrive on time blocking; others live by the Big Three. The key? Find your rhythm and stick to it consistently.

Option 1: Time Blocking

Best for: People who thrive on structure and like planned focus time.

- Allocate blocks of time for deep work, admin, and breaks.
- Helps protect your most productive hours.
- Reduces decision fatigue; you already know what you're doing.

Option 2: The Daily Big Three

Best for: People who need flexibility but still want focus.

- Each morning, pick the three most important things to accomplish.
- Forget long, overwhelming to-do lists.
- Keep your day focused and achievable.

Option: Combine The Two

- Combining the two methods can be incredibly effective, but it's not for everyone.
- Choose your daily Big Three, and block out time to complete them around your other commitments.

Rule: Pick the planning method that suits your personality. If it works, great; if not, change it up.

Step Five: Make It Sustainable

Even the best productivity system is useless if you don't stick with it.

Here's how to make sure your system lasts:

- **Do a quick daily check-in** – Review your tasks each morning.
- **Do a weekly reset** – Brain dump, filter tasks, and plan the next 7 days.
- **Stay flexible** – Adjust when things change instead of abandoning your system.

Your productivity system isn't set in stone; it's a tool that should evolve with you.

Final Thought: Productivity Should Work for You, Not the Other Way Around

The **DROP System** isn't about working harder; it's about working smarter.

By combining:

- A simple, effective toolset.
- A flexible workflow that adapts to your life.
- A ruthless focus on execution over perfection.

…you'll have a productivity system that actually works.

No more bouncing between different methods. No more wasting time tweaking systems instead of using them. Just a no-BS, practical way to stay on top of your work without burning out.

In the next section, we'll talk about how to make sure your system sticks, how to refine it over time, and what to do when things go off track.

Section 4: Your Productivity Playbook – Making It Stick

You've now got a personalised productivity system that works for you, not against you.

But here's the thing: A system is only as good as your ability to stick with it.

It's easy to feel motivated in the beginning, but the real challenge is making your system last beyond the initial burst of enthusiasm.

This section will cover:

- How to build consistency without feeling trapped by rigid routines.
- Why systems need to evolve over time.
- What to do when things inevitably go off track.

The Key to Long-Term Success: Make It Effortless

Most people fail at productivity not because they lack motivation but because their system requires too much effort.

If you have to:

- Spend an hour every day managing your to-do list... You won't stick to it.
- Rely on perfect discipline and willpower... You'll burn out.
- Follow a complicated routine that takes more time than it saves... You'll abandon it.

Rule: The easier your system is to maintain, the more likely you are to keep using it.

The **DROP System** is designed to be simple, flexible, and easy to maintain, so let's make sure you're applying it in a way that actually works long-term.

Build the Habit of a Daily & Weekly Review

The secret to keeping **any** productivity system running smoothly? Regular check-ins.

Daily Check-In (5 minutes max)

- Look at your task list. Is everything in the right place?
- Review your calendar; what's coming up today?
- Adjust if needed. Did something unexpected come up?

This stops your system from becoming cluttered or irrelevant.

Weekly Reset (20 minutes max)

- Do a full brain dump and get everything out of your head.
- Use **Delete, Delegate, and Do** to process tasks.
- Block time for important work or set your Daily Big Three for the week.

Rule: If you check your system daily and reset it weekly, **you'll never feel overwhelmed again.**

Expect and Plan for Things to Go Wrong

No matter how good your system is, life will throw curveballs.

- You'll have weeks where everything flows perfectly.
- And then you'll have weeks where everything implodes spectacularly.

What separates successful people from those who give up is the ability to reset and adapt instead of abandoning the system altogether.

How to Get Back on Track When You Fall Off

- **Wrong Approach:** "I missed a week, so I've failed."
- **Right Approach:** "I missed a week, so I'll reset today and keep going."
- **Wrong Approach:** "I forgot to check my to-do list, so I'll stop using it."
- **Right Approach:** "I forgot to check my to-do list, so I'll review it now and adjust."

Your system is there to **support you, not punish you.** If you fall off track, **just pick it back up.**

The DROP System is Meant to Evolve

Your productivity needs will change over time, so your system should, too.

- What works when you're busy might be too much when things slow down.
- What helps you stay on track now might feel restrictive later.
- Your goals, routines, and priorities will shift, so your system should adapt.

Rule: Productivity is a moving target, so keep refining and keep adjusting.

Questions to Ask Every Few Months:

- **What's working well?** – Keep it.
- **What feels like a chore?** – Simplify it.
- **Where am I procrastinating?** – Fix it.

The best productivity system isn't the one that looks good on paper, it's the one you'll still be using a year from now.

Final Thought: Make It Yours, Make It Work

At the end of the day, no system is perfect, but the DROP System is designed to be adaptable.

- **If something isn't working, change it.**
- **If you need more structure, add it.**
- **If you need more flexibility, allow it.**

This isn't about following a rigid method; it's about having a system that helps you get things done in a way that feels natural to you.

Now that you've got everything in place, the final step is learning how to start small and take action without getting stuck in overplanning mode.

That's exactly what we'll cover in the next section.

Section 5: The Final Step – Start Small & Take Action

You've got the tools. You've got the structure. You've got a system that actually works for you.

But here's where most people screw up: they overthink the execution.

They keep tweaking, planning, and perfecting but never actually start.

The final step in mastering the DROP System is simple: Start small. Take action. Stop overcomplicating.

The #1 Productivity Killer: Overplanning Instead of Doing

Here's the brutal truth:

Most people aren't stuck because they don't know what to do.

They're stuck because they're waiting for the perfect moment to start.

- "I need to get my to-do list organised first."
- "I should clean up my calendar before I begin."
- "Maybe I'll start fresh next week."

Bullshit.

If you're waiting for the perfect time, you'll be waiting forever.

Rule: Action beats planning. Always.

The Two-Minute Momentum Trick

The fastest way to break through hesitation is to lower the barrier to entry.

If a task feels overwhelming, shrink it down to the smallest possible action.

- Need to write a report? Open the document and write one sentence.
- Have emails piling up? Reply to just one.
- Need to sort your task list? Review three items, not the whole thing.

This is the Two-Minute Momentum Trick; start with something so small that you can't possibly fail.

Because once you've started, you're in motion, and momentum takes over.

The 80% Rule: Stop Aiming for Perfect, Aim for Done

Perfectionism is just procrastination in disguise.

- You don't need the perfect system; you just need one that works well enough.
- You don't need the perfect plan; you just need a rough direction.
- You don't need to get everything done; you just need to do the most important things.

Rule: If a task is 80% good enough, move on.

Nothing is ever perfect, and spending twice as long for a tiny improvement isn't worth it.

Build Your Execution Habit: How to Show Up Every Day

You don't need more motivation; you need better habits.

Here's how to make execution automatic:

1. Set an Unbreakable Daily Rule

Pick one small habit that keeps your system running.

Examples:

- Spend 3 minutes reviewing your task list.
- Brain dump before bed every night.
- Identify your block each morning.

2. Use the "No Zero Days" Mindset

A zero day is when you do nothing to move forward. The goal? Avoid them at all costs.

Even if you're exhausted, even if it's a bad day, do something.

- No time to exercise? Do five push-ups.
- Too busy to clean your inbox? Archive one email.
- No energy to write that report? Draft a single bullet point.

Rule: Tiny actions > No action at all.

3. End the Day With a Win

Before you wrap up each day, ask yourself:

"What's one thing I did today that moved me forward?"

Train your brain to focus on progress, not perfection.

Final Thought: The Best Productivity System is One You Actually Use

At this point, you've got everything you need to take control of your time and energy.

- You know how to clear mental clutter and focus on what matters.
- You've built a flexible, simple productivity system that fits your life.
- You've mastered the mindset and habits that will keep you on track.

Now, the only thing left to do?

Start.

No more overthinking. No more waiting for the perfect moment. No more bullshit.

Just start small, keep moving forward, and watch how much more you can get done without burning yourself out.

Chapter 9: Protecting Your Time

Section 1: The Harsh Reality – People Will Steal Your Time If You Let Them

By now, you've built a system that helps you get more done in less time, freeing up hours you never knew you had. But here's the brutal truth:

If you don't actively protect that time, someone else will take it.

It's not always intentional. Most people aren't deliberately trying to sabotage your productivity. But that doesn't stop them from pulling you into their distractions, their priorities, and their chaos.

Some people do it because they don't realise they're stealing your time.
Some do it because they don't respect boundaries.

And some do it because they're just selfish.

Regardless of the reason, if you let them, they will rob you of your most valuable asset.

This section is about identifying the time thieves in your life before they completely hijack your schedule.

Who Are the Biggest Time Thieves?

Most time thieves fall into three main categories:

Employees, Colleagues, and Team Members

- The **"Got a sec?" thief** – Constantly interrupts you with quick questions that turn into 30-minute discussions.
- The **"Can you check this?" thief** – Wants your approval on everything instead of making decisions themselves.
- The **"I didn't know what to do" thief** – Uses your time as a crutch instead of taking responsibility.

These people often mean well, but if you don't set boundaries, you'll spend your entire day micromanaging instead of focusing on your own work.

Bosses, Clients, and Business Contacts

- The **"Everything is urgent" thief** – Treats every request like a five-alarm fire, even when it's not.
- The **"Can you squeeze this in?" thief** – Sends last-minute requests with zero respect for your schedule.
- The **"Endless meeting" thief** – Calls unnecessary meetings that could've been an email.

If you're not careful, these people will dictate how you spend your time, leaving you with none for yourself.

Friends and Family – The Most Difficult Time Thieves to Manage

Here's where it gets tricky.

You can set boundaries with employees and colleagues. You can push back on clients. But family and friends?

That's where the guilt kicks in.

- "But it's just a quick favour."
- "You're always working; can't you take a break?"
- "I thought you'd want to spend time with us."

These are the people closest to you, which makes it ten times harder to say no.

But here's the problem: if you don't draw the line, they'll assume your time is always available.

Why Family and Friends Steal Your Time (Without Realising It)

Unlike colleagues or clients, family and friends:

- **Don't see your work the same way** – If you work from home or run your own business, they often assume you have "free time."

- **Expect instant availability** – They assume because they're close to you, they should come first, regardless of your workload.
- **Don't think about the consequences** – They don't realise that constant interruptions kill productivity and cause stress.

How to Handle It Without Damaging Relationships

The key is setting expectations early and enforcing them consistently:

- **Communicate your working hours** – Just because you're home doesn't mean you're available.
- **Create physical boundaries** – If your door is shut, you're off-limits. No exceptions.
- **Don't instantly reply** – Train people that you're not available 24/7 by delaying responses to non-urgent messages.
- **Schedule time together** – Instead of dropping everything when they demand attention, plan a proper time to be present.

It's not about shutting them out; it's about making sure they respect your time the same way they'd respect a regular 9-to-5 job.

The Psychology of Time Theft – Why People Take Your Time Without Thinking

The Convenience Factor

People will always take the path of least resistance; if you make yourself easily available, they'll use your time instead of solving their own problems.

The Lack of Consequence

If people interrupt you and you always drop everything to help, they learn that they can keep doing it without any pushback.

The Guilt Trap

Friends, family, and even colleagues will subconsciously play on guilt to get your time:

- *"But I really need your help with this."*
- *"I wouldn't ask if it wasn't important."*
- *"You're the only one who can do this."*

Reality check: Their lack of planning is not your emergency.

If you don't train people to value your time, they will keep stealing it.

Final Thought: People Will Treat Your Time How You Train Them To

If you act like your time is free and unlimited, people will treat it that way.

If you set boundaries and enforce them, people will learn to respect them.

Your time is yours. Guard it like your life depends on it, because in many ways, it does.

Section 2: The Golden Rule of Time Protection – Guard It Like a Limited Resource

Most people treat their time like it's limitless.

They act like they can always "make time" for one more thing, one more favour, one more meeting. But here's the reality:

- **You can't make more time.**
- **You can't buy more time.**
- **Once it's gone, it's gone.**

And yet, people hand it out freely, like it's worthless.

It's time to change that.

If you want to stay in control of your life, reduce stress, and actually enjoy the time you do have, you need to start treating your time like what it really is: your most valuable, non-renewable resource.

If Time Were Money, Would You Spend It This Carelessly?

Let's put it this way: Would you be broke if you handled your money the way you handled your time?

- Imagine if anyone could just take money from your wallet whenever they wanted.

- Imagine if you spent every penny on things you didn't actually need.
- Imagine if you woke up one day and realised you had nothing left to show for it.

That's exactly what happens with your time if you don't protect it.

Why People Respect Money More Than Time (and Why That's Backwards)

- People know that money runs out.
- People feel the loss of money immediately, but they don't feel lost time the same way.
- Society has conditioned us to be stingy with money but generous with time.

But remember this: You can always earn more money, but you'll never get back wasted time.

The Shift You Need to Make Right Now

Instead of thinking, "How can I fit more in?" start thinking ", How can I protect my time like I protect my bank account?"

Because when you start treating your time like money, you'll naturally:

- Say no to pointless meetings and distractions.
- Be more intentional with how you spend your day.
- Stop letting people "borrow" your time without a return on investment.

The Reality Check: Every "Yes" is a Trade-Off

Every time you say **yes** to something, you're saying **no** to something else.

- **Say yes to another pointless meeting?** You're saying no to deep work time.
- **Say yes to every favour from a friend.** You're saying no to time for yourself.
- **Say yes to working late every night?** You're saying no to your personal life.

Rule: Every **yes** costs you something. Make sure it's worth it.

Before you agree to anything, ask yourself:

- *Does this align with my priorities?*
- *If I say yes, what am I saying no to?*
- *Would I still say yes if this cost me actual money?*

If the answer isn't a **clear yes**, it's a **sorry but no**.

The Art of Saying No (Without the Guilt)

A lot of people struggle to say no because they don't want to seem rude or unhelpful.

But here's the truth: Successful people aren't afraid to say no.

If you say yes to everything:

- You'll be buried in other people's priorities.
- You'll have zero time left for what actually matters.
- You'll be resentful, exhausted, and constantly behind.

How to Say No (Without Sounding Like a Twat)

The "I'm Booked" No:

"I'd love to help, but my schedule is completely full right now."

The Deferral No:

"I can't take this on right now, but let's check back in next month."

The Prioritisation No:

"If I do this, I'll have to push something else back; what should we deprioritise?"

The Flat-Out No (For Persistent Time Thieves):

"I'm not available for this; thanks for understanding."

The more you practice saying no, the easier it gets.

Rule: Your time is yours; act like it.

How to Audit Your Time (And Cut the Dead Weight)

If you're constantly overwhelmed, chances are you're spending time on things that don't actually matter.

Here's how to do a quick time audit and cut the dead weight:

Step 1: Track Your Time for One Week

- Write down everything you do for a week.
- Be brutally honest, including wasting time on distractions and unnecessary tasks.

Step 2: Identify Your "Time Leaks"

Look at your log and ask:

- *What tasks are eating up the most time?*
- *What can I delete, delegate, or automate?*
- *What should I be spending MORE time on?*

Step 3: Cut the Dead Weight

- **Delete** pointless meetings, busy work, and obligations that add no value.
- **Delegate** anything someone else can do.
- **Automate** recurring tasks to free up time.

Rule: If it doesn't move you forward, cut it.

Final Thought: Time is Your Most Valuable Asset, Guard It Like It Matters

Your time is the most valuable thing you own.

If you don't start protecting it, someone else will keep taking it.

- Start treating time like money.
- Understand that every yes is a trade-off.
- Learn to say no without guilt.
- Audit your time and cut the waste.

Because once you start guarding your time like it actually matters, everything changes.

Section 4: Managing Interruptions Like a Pro

Even if you've set boundaries and trained people to respect your time, interruptions will still happen.

That's because interruptions don't just come from other people; they also come from you.

- **External interruptions** – Employees, clients, colleagues, family, notifications, emails.
- **Internal interruptions** – Your own bad habits, distractions, lack of focus, procrastination.

Interruptions aren't just annoying; they're productivity killers. Studies show that it takes 23 minutes to fully refocus after a distraction. Multiply that by a dozen daily interruptions, and half your workday is wasted before you know it.

This section is all about eliminating distractions, controlling interruptions, and staying focused without feeling like a prisoner to your schedule.

Identify Your Biggest Distractions (External vs. Internal)

Before you can fix the problem, you need to know where your interruptions are coming from.

External Interruptions (Other People Stealing Your Focus)

- "Got a sec?" coworkers who turn into a 20-minute chat.
- Clients who expect instant replies.
- Family members who assume you're free just because you're home.
- Endless emails, Slack messages, and notifications.

Internal Interruptions (You Stealing Your Own Focus)

- Mindlessly checking your phone every five minutes.
- Bouncing between tasks instead of finishing one.

- Procrastinating on high-value work by doing low-value tasks instead.
- Getting sucked into "fake work" that makes you feel busy but achieves nothing.

Rule: Not all distractions come from other people; sometimes, you're your own worst enemy.

The 3-Step Formula to Managing External Interruptions

Step 1: Block Interruptions Before They Happen

- Set **Do Not Disturb** on your phone and computer during deep work sessions.
- **Turn off email and Slack notifications**; check them on your schedule, not someone else's.
- Use **"Office Hours"** – Let people know when you're available (and when you're not).
- Physically **close your door or wear headphones** – A universal "Do Not Disturb" signal.

Step 2: Control How People Access You

If you're always available, people will keep interrupting you.

- **Set response time expectations:** *"I check emails twice a day; expect a reply within 24 hours."*
- **Batch communication:** Instead of responding all day, set fixed times for checking messages.
- **Use a gatekeeper (if possible):** If you have an assistant, let them filter low-priority requests.

Step 3: Train People to Respect Your Time

If someone keeps interrupting despite clear boundaries, redirect them with a simple rule:

The "Send It to Me" Rule

"I can't chat right now, but send it over, and I'll check it when I have time."

The "Solution First" Rule

"What do you think we should do? Come back with a solution, and we'll discuss it."

The "Let's Schedule It" Rule

"Let's set a proper time to go through this instead of rushing it now."

Rule: If you don't set the standard, people will keep interrupting you whenever they want.

The 3-Step Formula to Managing Internal Distractions

Your phone isn't the problem.

Your email isn't the problem.

Your procrastination isn't the problem.

Your inability to control them is!

Here's how to fix it.

Step 1: Fix Your Environment

Your brain is lazy; it will default to the easiest option (which is usually a distraction).

- **Remove temptations:** Keep your phone in another room if you don't need it.
- **Set up your workspace:** A cluttered desk leads to a cluttered mind.
- **Use website blockers:** If you keep checking social media, block it during work hours.

Step 2: Use Time Blocking to Force Focus

We've already covered time blocking earlier in the book, but this is where it becomes non-negotiable.

- **Block out deep work time** – Treat it like a meeting you can't skip.

- **Use a visible timer** – Set it for 60-90 minutes and commit to no distractions.
- **Batch shallow work together** – Emails, admin, and small tasks should be grouped, not spread throughout the day.

Step 3: Break the "Instant Gratification" Habit

Most distractions happen because your brain wants quick dopamine hits.

- Scrolling social media feels easier than deep work.
- Checking emails feels easier than tackling big projects.
- Bouncing between tasks feels productive but achieves nothing.

To stop this, use the 5-Minute Rule:

- Commit to working for just 5 minutes before allowing yourself a distraction.
- By the time the 5 minutes are up, you'll usually be in the zone.

Rule: The less friction between you and deep work, the easier it is to stay focused.

What to Do When Interruptions Are Unavoidable

No matter how good your system is, some interruptions can't be avoided.

Here's how to handle them without losing focus completely.

Option 1: The "Pause and Resume" Method

If you get interrupted in the middle of deep work:

- Write down exactly what you were doing before the interruption.
- When you return, use that note to immediately pick up where you left off.
- This reduces the time it takes to refocus after an interruption.

Option 2: The "Buffer Time" Strategy

If your job involves regular interruptions (e.g., managing a team), schedule buffer time into your day.

- Instead of trying to work uninterrupted for 8 hours, plan for interruptions.
- Have two or three designated times per day when you're available for questions, meetings, or unexpected issues.

Option 3: The "Not Right Now" Approach

If someone interrupts you with a non-urgent request, don't drop everything; instead, say:

"I'm in the middle of something; let's come back to this at [specific time]."

Most of the time? They'll figure it out without you.

Final Thought: Your Attention is Your Power, Protect It at All Costs

Distractions aren't just stealing your time; they're stealing your ability to focus on what truly matters.

- If you don't block interruptions, people will keep taking your time.
- If you don't control distractions, they will control you.
- If you don't train your brain to focus, you'll constantly feel scattered.

Master your interruptions, and you master your time.

Master your time, and you master your results.

Now, in the final section of this chapter, we're going to cover one last skill: the ability to walk away from the worst time thieves in your life.

Conclusion: The Ultimate Truth About Productivity

If there's one thing you take away from this book, let it be this:

Working harder is NOT the answer.

You've been sold the myth that success comes from grinding longer hours, hustling harder, and pushing through exhaustion.

But now, you know the truth.

- Being busy is not the same as being productive.
- Long hours don't guarantee success; they guarantee burnout.
- Trying to "outwork" the chaos will only keep you stuck in it.

The real secret? Doing what matters consistently.

The DROP System: The Only Productivity System You'll Ever Need

This book hasn't been about working more. It's been about working smarter.

And that's exactly why you now have the **DROP System**, a no-BS, flexible framework that actually works:

- **Brain Dump Everything** – Get everything out of your head and into a system.
- **Delete, Delegate, Do** – Ruthlessly filter what matters and ditch the rest.
- **Time Block or Use the Daily Big Three** – Control your schedule instead of reacting to it.
- **Protect Your Time** – If you don't guard your time, someone else will take it.

This isn't just a system; it's a mindset shift.

Because once you stop wasting time on the wrong things, you'll be shocked at how much time you actually have.

The Harsh Truth: If You Don't Protect Your Time, No One Else Will

Let's be blunt:

- No one is coming to save your schedule.
- If you don't set boundaries, people will keep stealing your time.
- If you don't change how you operate, nothing in your life will change.

The reason most people stay overwhelmed, exhausted, and stuck is simple:

They let other people's priorities run their lives instead of taking control.

But you? You know better now.

And now it's time to act on it.

Your Final Challenge: Stop Wasting Time on the Wrong Things

This isn't just about productivity; it's about taking back control of your time, energy, and life.

So here's my challenge to you:

- **Take one action today**, right now that will protect your time.
- Say no to something that doesn't serve you.
- Cut out a task, a habit, or a distraction that's been wasting your energy.

- Protect one deep work session for tomorrow
- Identify the biggest time thief, and tell them "No."

Because the second you start prioritising what actually matters, everything changes.

Your Time, Your Choice

If you've made it this far, you already know the truth: working harder isn't the answer.

You've seen how productivity myths keep people trapped in cycles of stress and burnout. You've learned how to build a system that works for you—not against you. And most importantly, you now understand that protecting your time isn't a luxury—it's a necessity.

The question is: **what happens next?**

Because here's the reality—most people will close this book, agree with everything they've just read, and then go straight back to business as usual. They'll keep saying yes to everything, letting distractions dictate their days, and putting off the changes they know they need to make.

But you're not most people.

If there's one thing I hope this book has given you, it's the permission to take control of your time. To stop letting guilt, pressure, and other people's demands run your life. To be intentional about how you spend your time, so you can create more of it for what actually matters—to you.

This is your call to action, but it's not mine to give. It's yours. Your time. Your choice.

If you're ready to go deeper, refine your systems, or get tailored support in implementing everything you've learned, you'll find additional tools, resources, and ways to work with me in the Services Offered by The Author section. Whether it's coaching, workshops, or practical training, these are there to help you keep moving forward.

Because time is the one thing you can never get back.

Go use yours wisely.

Appendix 1: Additional Resources and Tools

Throughout this book, we've covered practical strategies to help you master productivity, protect your time, and get more done without burning yourself out.

But learning doesn't stop here. The right tools and resources can make the difference between knowing what to do and actually implementing it.

This appendix provides a curated list of the most effective:

- Task and project management tools
- Time blocking and scheduling apps
- Distraction blockers and focus tools
- Books and podcasts for deeper learning

If you want to fully integrate the **DROP System** into your daily life, this is where to start.

Task & Project Management Tools

One of the biggest barriers to productivity is not knowing where to store and track your tasks.

A brain dump is only effective if you have a system to organise and execute it. That's where these tools come in.

Best for Personal Task Management

- **Todoist** – A simple and effective app for managing personal to-do lists.
- **Microsoft To Do** – Syncs across devices integrates with Outlook, and keeps lists structured.
- **Google Task** – Syncs across devices, integrates with Outlook, and keeps lists structured.
- **Google Keep** – Great for quick notes and reminders.

Best for Project & Team Management

- **ClickUp** – Highly customisable, integrates with other tools, and scales from personal use to enterprise-level teams.
- **Trello** – A visual, card-based system perfect for workflow and project tracking.
- **Notion** – A flexible all-in-one workspace for notes, tasks, and team collaboration.
- **Asana** – Great for tracking tasks, deadlines, and projects in teams.

Best for Habit & Routine Tracking

- **Habitica** – Turns habit-building into a game for those who need motivation.
- **Streaks** – Simple, visual habit tracker for iOS users.
- **Loop Habit Tracker** – A free, data-driven habit tracker for Android.

Time Blocking & Scheduling Tools

Time blocking isn't just a technique; it's a discipline.

Using the right tools ensures that your time blocks don't get hijacked by distractions or reactive work.

Best for Calendar-Based Time Blocking

- **Google Calendar** – A staple for scheduling deep work, meetings, and recurring tasks.
- **Sunsama** – A daily planner that integrates time blocking with task management.
- **Reclaim.ai** – An AI-powered calendar that auto-schedules tasks and meetings.

Best for Time Tracking & Optimisation

- **RescueTime** – Tracks how you actually spend your time on devices.
- **Toggl** – A simple, manual time-tracking tool for accountability.
- **Clockify** – A free alternative for tracking work hours and tasks.

Distraction Management & Deep Work Tools

Eliminating distractions is non-negotiable if you want to work at peak performance. These tools will help block interruptions and create an environment for focus.

Website & App Blockers

- **Freedom** – Blocks distracting websites and apps across all devices.
- **Cold Turkey** – A stricter alternative that locks distractions completely.
- **StayFocusd (Chrome Extension)** – Limits time spent on time-wasting sites.

Focus & Noise Control

- **Brain.fm** – AI-generated music scientifically designed to enhance focus.
- **Noisli** – Custom background noise generator for deep work sessions.
- **Krisp.ai** – AI-powered noise cancellation for calls and meetings.

Proven Productivity Techniques & Their Tools

Many of the concepts in this book are based on tried-and-tested productivity methods. Here's a refresher on some of the most effective techniques, along with tools to implement them.

The Pomodoro Technique (Work in Short, Focused Sprints)

Concept: Work for **25 minutes**, take a **5-minute break**, repeat. Every four cycles, take a longer break.

Why It Works: Helps fight procrastination and keeps focus high.

Best Tools:

- **Pomodone** – Combines the Pomodoro technique with task management.
- **Be Focused** – A simple Pomodoro timer for Mac users.

- **Marinara Timer (Web-Based)** – Free online Pomodoro tracker.

The Eisenhower Matrix (Deciding What's Important vs. Urgent)

Concept: Categorise tasks into four quadrants:

1. **Urgent & Important** – Do these immediately.
2. **Important, Not Urgent** – Schedule these for later (often deep work).
3. **Urgent, Not Important** – Delegate or automate.
4. **Neither Urgent nor Important** – Delete entirely.

Best Tools:

- **Priority Matrix** – Helps organise tasks based on urgency vs. importance.
- **Eisenhower App** – A dedicated tool for managing priorities visually.

The 5 AM Club (Waking Early to Own Your Day)

Concept: A routine from Robin Sharma's book, where you wake at 5 AM to focus on personal growth, deep work, and mindfulness before the world wakes up.

Why It's Controversial: Works brilliantly for early risers but forces night owls into unnatural routines. (*We covered why rigid systems like this don't work for everyone in Chapter 6.*)

Best Tools for Morning Productivity:

- **Sleep Cycle** – Smart alarm that wakes you at the lightest sleep stage.
- **Morning!** – A structured morning routine planner.
- **Fabulous** – Habit-building app that helps structure a strong morning routine.

Brain Dumping (Getting Mental Clutter onto Paper)

Concept: Write down everything in your head: tasks, ideas, and worries, then sort it into a system.

Best Tools:

- **Notion or Evernote** – Great for digital brain dumping.
- **Bullet Journaling** – For those who prefer analogue systems.
- **Apple Notes or Google Keep** – Simple, no-frills note-taking apps.

Getting Things Done – David Allen

Concept: Capture everything, clarify what's actionable, organise it, reflect regularly, and execute.

Best Tools:

- **OmniFocus** – Best for hardcore GTD users.
- **Things 3** – A simplified GTD approach.
- **Evernote** – Great for GTD-style task organisation.

A Quick Note on Tools & Apps

Throughout this book, I've mentioned various tools, apps, and software that can help streamline your productivity. But here's the reality—technology changes, companies pivot, and tools come and go. What's here today might be obsolete tomorrow.

The key takeaway isn't the specific tools themselves—it's the function they serve. Whether it's a task manager, a habit tracker, or an automation tool, there will always be an alternative that does the same job (if not better). The principle remains the same—find a tool that works for you, use it well, and don't get too attached.

I can't control whether an app shuts down, changes its pricing, or gets acquired by a bigger company that ruins it. But what I can give you are the right strategies, systems, and habits—ones that will keep working no matter what tools are available.

Final Thoughts: Choose the Right Tools, But Don't Overcomplicate

Having the right tools and frameworks will make your productivity system easier to implement and maintain.

BUT, be careful.

- Don't spend more time "optimising" your tools than actually doing the work.
- Don't use five different apps when one would do.
- Don't let productivity tools become a distraction themselves.
- The best tool is the one you actually use.

Appendix 2: Further Reading Recommendations

This book has given you my no-nonsense approach to time management, productivity, and discipline.

But if you want to go deeper, there are countless books that explore specific areas, from eliminating distractions to building better habits.

This appendix is your reading list for levelling up.

Every book here has influenced the ideas, strategies, and techniques in this book. Some are classics, and some are newer, but all of them will make you think differently about how you use your time.

Books on Productivity & Time Management

These books focus on **working smarter, not harder**, and will help reinforce the strategies covered in this book.

The One Thing – Gary Keller

- The power of focusing on one high-impact task instead of juggling too many.
- A great read if you struggle with prioritisation and deep work.

Deep Work – Cal Newport

- Why distraction is killing your ability to focus and how to rebuild it.
- A must-read if you want to master undistracted, high-quality work.

Essentialism – Greg McKeown

- The ruthless art of saying no to anything that doesn't matter.
- Ideal if you need help cutting out unnecessary obligations.

Make Time – Jake Knapp & John Zeratsky

- How to control your daily schedule instead of reacting to distractions.
- A great book if you want practical, easy-to-apply strategies.

The 12-Week Year – Brian Moran

- Why yearly goals are ineffective and how to plan in 12-week cycles instead.
- Perfect for those who struggle to stay on track with long-term goals.

The 4-Hour Workweek – Tim Ferriss

- A radical rethink of traditional work structures and time freedom.
- Great for entrepreneurs who want to work less but achieve more.

Books on Procrastination & Discipline

Procrastination is a psychological battle. These books explain why you put things off and how to fix it.

The War of Art – Steven Pressfield

- How to overcome resistance and get things done, even when you don't feel like it.
- A powerful read for anyone who struggles with self-discipline.

The Willpower Instinct – Kelly McGonigal

- The science behind why willpower fails and how to strengthen it.
- Great for those who struggle with staying consistent.

Mindset – Carol S. Dweck

- The difference between a fixed mindset (failure is permanent) and a growth mindset (failure is feedback).
- A must-read for shifting how you approach challenges.

The Now Habit – Neil Fiore

- A deep dive into why we procrastinate and how to stop.
- Perfect if you need a structured approach to breaking bad habits.

Atomic Habits – James Clear

- How small, consistent habits lead to massive long-term success.
- Essential reading for anyone who wants to build better habits.

The 5-Second Rule – Mel Robbins

- A simple trick to override hesitation and take action immediately.
- Great for those who struggle with overthinking and self-doubt.

Books on Boundaries, Saying No, and Protecting Your Time

If you struggle with setting boundaries, saying no, and protecting your schedule, these books will help.

The Subtle Art of Not Giving a F*ck – Mark Manson

- A brutally honest take on prioritising what truly matters.
- Great for those who worry too much about what others think.

Set Boundaries, Find Peace – Nedra Glover Tawwab

- Practical steps for setting clear boundaries without guilt.
- A must-read for anyone who struggles to say no.

Boundaries – Dr. Henry Cloud & Dr. John Townsend

- Why boundaries are essential for mental health and productivity.
- Perfect if you need real-world scripts for enforcing boundaries.

Digital Minimalism – Cal Newport

- How to reclaim your focus by reducing digital distractions.
- Essential reading for those addicted to social media and notifications.

Stolen Focus – Johann Hari

- A deep dive into why our attention spans are shrinking and how to take back control.
- Great if you feel constantly distracted.

Books on Sleep, Energy, and Biological Rhythms

Productivity isn't just about what you do; it's also about how well you recover.

Why We Sleep – Matthew Walker

- The science of sleep and how it impacts focus, memory, and productivity.
- A must-read if you think sleep is optional (it's not).

The Circadian Code – Satchin Panda

- How your body clock affects energy, focus, and health.
- Great for optimising your daily routine based on biology.

Own the Day, Own Your Life – Aubrey Marcus

- How to structure your mornings, work, nutrition, and movement for peak performance.
- Perfect if you want a holistic approach to productivity.

The 5 AM Club – Robin Sharma

- A structured morning routine for high-performance habits.
- While effective for early risers, it's NOT for everyone (*as we covered in Chapter 6*).

The Power of When – Dr. Michael Breus

- How to discover your chronotype and structure your schedule accordingly.
- A must-read if you want to work with your natural rhythms, not against them.

Books on Leadership, Focus, and Decision-Making

Success isn't just about doing more; it's about making better decisions and managing time like a leader.

Extreme Ownership – Jocko Willink

- A Navy SEAL's guide to taking full responsibility for time and priorities.
- Essential reading for leaders and business owners.

The Effective Executive – Peter Drucker

- A classic on how top performers manage time and decision-making.
- Great if you want to level up your leadership skills.

Measure What Matters – John Doerr

- How to set OKRs (Objectives & Key Results) for high-impact goals.
- A must-read if you want to track progress effectively.

The 80/20 Principle – Richard Koch

- Why 80% of results come from 20% of effort.
- A game-changer for cutting out unnecessary work.

Final Thought: The Best Learning Never Stops

This book has given you the **DROP System** and the tools to take control of your time, focus, and productivity.

But true mastery comes from continuous learning.

If you want to go deeper:

- Pick one book from this list that resonates with you.
- Start reading it within the next week.
- Apply at least one principle from it to your daily routine.

Because at the end of the day, knowledge is useless unless you take action.

Appendix 3: Acknowledgements And Bibliography

Acknowledgements

No book is written in isolation. While the words in these pages are mine, the lessons, insights, and experiences that shaped them came from many people along the way.

First off, **to my clients**—you know who you are. Every challenge, frustration, and breakthrough you've shared with me over the years has shaped the ideas in this book. You're the reason this system exists. Watching you struggle through chaos, push past overwhelm, and finally get your time back has been my greatest motivation.

To my **friends and family**—thanks for putting up with me while I disappeared into writing mode. Writing a book on productivity and time management while ignoring social plans and snapping at interruptions? The irony wasn't lost on me. Appreciate you all for understanding.

A huge shoutout to **Danielle**, my wife and partner in crime. Sixteen years, and you still haven't kicked me out—I think that deserves some kind of award. Your patience, support, and ability to put up with my obsession with refining systems (even when it leaks into home life) mean everything.

To my **daughters, Charlotte and Amelia**—you two are the best reminders that balance isn't just some productivity buzzword. Watching you grow up made me realise that time is the most valuable thing we have and that no amount of 'hard work' is worth missing out on what really matters.

To **Alan Brighton**, my first business coach—thanks for tearing down my self-imposed limits and showing me how to rebuild myself as a stronger leader. If you hadn't pushed me to step up, this book wouldn't exist.

And finally, to **you, the reader**. If you made it this far, I know you're serious about getting your time back and finally breaking free from the grind. This book means nothing if it just sits on your shelf. **Use it. Implement it. Own your time.**

Because at the end of the day, time is the only thing you can never get back.

Now, go protect yours.

Bibliography & References

This book draws from a combination of personal experience, time-tested productivity systems, and research-backed strategies. Below is a complete list of the sources, studies, and frameworks referenced throughout.

Books Referenced

Atomic Habits – James Clear (*How small, consistent habits create massive results.*)
Deep Work – Cal Newport (*Mastering focus in a distracted world.*)
The One Thing – Gary Keller (*Prioritising the highest-impact tasks.*)
Essentialism – Greg McKeown (*Eliminating non-essential work and distractions.*)
The 12-Week Year – Brian Moran (*Why shorter planning cycles beat annual goals.*)
The 4-Hour Workweek – Tim Ferriss (*Escaping the cycle of traditional work structures.*)
The War of Art – Steven Pressfield (*Overcoming resistance and procrastination.*)
The Willpower Instinct – Kelly McGonigal (*How self-control works and how to strengthen it.*)
Mindset – Carol S. Dweck (*The difference between a fixed and growth mindset.*)
The Now Habit – Neil Fiore (*Understanding why we procrastinate and how to stop.*)
The Subtle Art of Not Giving a F*ck – Mark Manson (*Learning to prioritise what truly matters.*)
Set Boundaries, Find Peace – Nedra Glover Tawwab (*Practical boundary-setting strategies.*)
Digital Minimalism – Cal Newport (*Reducing digital distractions for better focus.*)
Stolen Focus – Johann Hari (*Why modern distractions are killing our attention spans.*)
Why We Sleep – Matthew Walker (*The science of sleep and its impact on productivity.*)
The Circadian Code – Satchin Panda (*Understanding biological rhythms for peak performance.*)
Own the Day, Own Your Life – Aubrey Marcus (*Structuring your day for optimal energy and focus.*)

The 5 AM Club – Robin Sharma (*A morning routine framework for high performance.*)
The Power of When – Dr. Michael Breus (*Discovering your personal productivity rhythm.*)
Extreme Ownership – Jocko Willink (*The discipline of time management from a leadership perspective.*)
The Effective Executive – Peter Drucker (*Classic insights on how top performers manage time and decisions.*)
Measure What Matters – John Doerr (*Setting and tracking OKRs for high-impact goals.*)
The 80/20 Principle – Richard Koch (*Why 80% of results come from 20% of effort.*)
Four Thousand Weeks – Oliver Burkeman (*Why, given out limited time upon this earth, do we focus on doing more work.*)

Studies & Research Referenced

American Psychological Association (APA) – Research on multitasking, cognitive overload, and willpower depletion.

Harvard Business Review – Multiple studies on focus, deep work, and the effects of interruptions.

Stanford University – Research on task switching and why multitasking destroys productivity.

University of California, Irvine – Study on how long it takes to refocus after an interruption (23 minutes, on average).

The Pomodoro Technique – Francesco Cirillo – The science behind working in **focused time sprints** and why breaks boost productivity.
The Eisenhower Matrix – President Dwight D. Eisenhower – The prioritisation method separating urgent vs. important tasks.

Parkinson's Law – Cyril Northcote Parkinson – The concept that work expands to fill the time available for its completion.

Circadian Rhythms – National Institute of General Medical Sciences – How biological clocks impact energy levels and focus.

Final, Final Thought: Knowledge is Useless Without Action

This book is packed with actionable strategies, proven techniques, and research-backed insights. But none of it matters unless you do something with it.

Pick your systems. Implement them. Protect your time.

Your future self will thank you.

About the Author

Adam Fox's journey with time and productivity didn't start in a boardroom or on a stage. It started at age 12, at 6 AM, in a freezing cold newsagents, folding newspapers before the school bus arrived.

At just 12 years old, he had the longest paper round in the village—for the lowest pay. When he questioned why, the 90-year-old newsagent told him, "That's just the way it is." Adam had two choices: accept it or find a way to make it work. So he did what would become second nature to him throughout his life—he found a smarter way.

That lesson—figuring out how to get the best return for his effort—would follow him through every stage of his career.

From there, the relentless work ethic continued. Pot washing at 14. Stacking supermarket shelves at 15. At 16, when most of his mates were figuring out how to do the least work possible, Adam was juggling school with working every legal hour available to save up for a World Challenge expedition. He quickly learned the power of strategic effort—putting energy into what gets results rather than just burning yourself out for the sake of it.

After taking a year out between sixth form and university, Adam travelled the world with two friends—an experience that opened his eyes to the possibilities beyond the traditional education-to-career pipeline. When he returned, university was no longer the obvious next step. Instead, his HR manager and store manager convinced him to skip the student loans and go straight into a management training scheme. Looking at the numbers, it was a no-brainer—why spend three years in a classroom when he could be learning (and earning) in the real world?

That first big career decision taught Adam something crucial: success isn't about following someone else's script—it's about making the right moves for your own journey. But it also revealed what wasn't right for him. He excelled in management, but the corporate environment—stuck in an office, following rigid processes—suffocated him. He wanted to be out in the world, meeting people and seeing new places.

So, he left and retrained as an asbestos consultant. It was a far cry from supermarket management, but it gave him the mobility and variety he craved. He excelled in the field, building up expertise and gaining respect quickly, but a harsh reality set in—he was being severely underpaid. New trainees were being hired for more money than him. That was the final straw. He walked.

That decision led him to a great company, one where he finally felt valued. But when that company merged with a corporate giant, everything changed overnight. The culture shift was unbearable—suddenly, the focus was more on spreadsheets and politics than actually getting things done. It was time to move on again.

That's when Adam and his dad went into business together. It should have been the perfect move—family, experience, and a shared goal. However, it quickly became apparent that they had very different ideas about business, growth, and marketing. Rather than risk damaging the most important relationship in his life, Adam chose to walk away.

From there, he stepped into the corporate world one final time—going from surveyor to project manager, operations manager, operations director, and finally to managing director. It was a rapid rise, and on paper, it looked like the dream career trajectory. But something was missing. He was running on empty.

Then, everything changed. He became a father.

Suddenly, the long hours, the late nights, the constant firefighting at work—it wasn't just exhausting. It was stealing time from the people who needed him most. His colleagues, his boss, his clients… they all got the best of him, while his family got the exhausted, distracted, running-on-fumes version. That wasn't good enough.

That's when the search for a better way became non-negotiable.

Adam went all in. He read everything he could on time management, productivity, psychology, neuroscience—devouring every study, every book, every framework he could get his hands on. Not to be more efficient at work but to create more time for his family.

What he found was a brutal truth: most productivity advice is complete rubbish.

- "Just wake up at 5 AM!" – Great if you're an early bird. Torture if you're not.
- "Hustle harder!" I already tried that. Nearly wrecked himself in the process.
- "Follow this one-size-fits-all system, and you'll be successful!" – Productivity isn't universal. It's personal.

So, he started testing, refining, and developing his own system—one that actually worked. A system that didn't just help him get more done but helped him protect his time so he could be fully present for his family while still growing a successful business.

He left the corporate world for good and threw himself into business coaching, productivity, and time management. He realised that most business owners weren't failing because they weren't working hard enough—they were failing because they were working on the wrong things in the wrong way.

Through his coaching business, **Evolve,** Adam has helped countless business owners and professionals escape the same trap he was once stuck in. He teaches them how to:

- Master their time without working longer hours.
- Build businesses that don't rely on them being constantly "on."
- Stop drowning in tasks and start making real progress.

This book isn't just a collection of theories. It's built on experience—real lessons learned through years of trial and error and figuring out how to reclaim time without sacrificing success.

Because if there's one thing Adam knows for certain, it's this: Productivity isn't about doing more—it's about creating time for what matters most.

Services Offered by the Author

I don't just write about productivity—I live and breathe it. My mission isn't just to share theories; it's to help business owners, entrepreneurs, and professionals master time management, productivity, and focus in real life.

Because reading about productivity is one thing, implementing it is another.

If you're serious about taking back control of your time, your workload, and your results, here's how I can help through The DORP System & Evolve Business Coaching with my productivity and business strategy services:

Business Coaching & Strategy – Get Your Business Working for YOU

Your business should give you freedom, not chain you to an endless cycle of stress and firefighting. Through **Evolve Business Coaching**, I help business owners escape the grind, scale their businesses without working longer hours, and build a business that actually works for them.

1:1 Business & Productivity Coaching – Strategy, Execution & Accountability

If you're overwhelmed, stretched too thin, and struggling to scale your business without working longer hours, this is for you.

- A personalised productivity & business strategy—built around how YOU work best.
- Time & task management systems—no more firefighting, just clarity and focus.
- **A**ccountability & execution coaching—because knowing what to do isn't enough; you need to actually do it.
- A plan to stop time-wasting tasks—so you can focus on growth, profit, and impact.

If you want to stop feeling like your business is running you instead of the other way around, we'll fix that—fast.

Business Strategy Planning – Get Clear on the Big Picture

Sometimes, you need to zoom out before you can move forward. If you're feeling stuck in the day-to-day grind, struggling to see the bigger picture, or trying to scale without burning out, a Business Strategy Planning session will give you the clarity, structure, and direction you need.

- Deep dive into your business model, goals, and bottlenecks.
- Identify the key areas holding you back.
- Develop a practical, no-nonsense plan to move forward with clear priorities.
- Break down your strategy into actionable steps, so you stop overthinking and start executing.

This isn't just about productivity—it's about creating a business that works for you, not the other way around.

Business Growth Coaching – Move from Hustle to Scalability

If you're serious about scaling your business but feel like you're stuck in the daily grind, it's time to shift from working IN your business to working ON your business. This coaching focuses on:

- Building systems so your business runs smoothly without you doing everything.
- Hiring & delegation—how to build a team that actually lightens your load.
- Shifting from being a worker to a business owner.
- Long-term strategy & execution support.

If you've built a business but still feel like an employee in it, we'll fix that and get you back in control.

Intensive Business Coaching Programmes – Accelerate Your Results

For business owners who need a short, sharp intervention to get unstuck and move fast, I offer:

The "Coaching Kickstart" Programme – A 6-week intensive coaching plan designed to give you clarity, direction, and momentum—perfect if you're unsure whether long-term coaching is for you.

The "Get Your Big Idea Done" Programme – A 12-week sprint to finally execute that project, launch, or system you've been putting off.

If you've got a big idea, a stalled project, or an overwhelming to-do list, this programme will get you moving—fast.

Workshops & Keynotes – No-Nonsense Talks That Get Results

I deliver high-impact, straight-talking workshops and keynotes on:

- **Time management**—how to take control of your schedule instead of letting others hijack it.
- **Productivity**—real-world strategies to get more done in less time.
- **Procrastination**—why we do it and how to stop it for good.
- **Discipline over motivation**—how to get things done even when you don't feel like it.
- **Business growth strategies**—practical frameworks to scale without burning out.

I've worked with businesses, leadership teams, networking groups, and conferences to help people ditch the productivity myths and start working smarter.

If you need a speaker or trainer who will cut through the fluff and actually get your audience to take action, let's talk.

Online Training & Resources – Get Productive at Your Own Pace

Let's face it: not everyone has the time, money, or appetite for 1:1 coaching or live workshops. That's why I've built self-paced training, practical guides, and frameworks to help you implement everything in this book.

- Step-by-step online courses—so you can learn and apply productivity techniques at your own pace.
- Downloadable frameworks—plug-and-play systems to help you manage your time and workload.
- Exclusive content—deep dives into procrastination, focus, and high-performance habits.

If you want to level up your productivity on your own terms, my online resources give you the tools to take action whenever you're ready.

If you're serious about transforming how you work and live, I can help you cut through the noise, focus on what matters, and finally take control of your time and business.

Let's make it happen.

Contact Details

📞 **Telephone**: +44 7305828625
✉ **Email**: adam@thedropsystem.co.uk
✉ **Email**: adam@evolvebusinesscoaching.co.uk
🌐 **Website**: www.thedropsystem.co.uk
🌐 **Website**: www.evolvebusinesscoaching.co.uk

Follow me on social media for no-nonsense productivity insights:

LinkedIn: www.linkedin.com/in/adam-fox-coach
LinkedIn: www.linkedin.com/company/the-drop-system

Scan the QR code to find all my contact details and links in 1 place:

Got questions? Want to work together? **Reach out—I'd love to hear from you.**

One More Thing Before You Go...

If you enjoyed reading this book or found it useful, I'd be very grateful if you'd post a short review on Amazon.
Your support really does make a difference, and I read all the reviews personally, so I can get your feedback and make this book even better.

If you would like to leave a review, then all you need to do is click the review link on Amazon here:
You will be shown how to get your review links to place here.

Thanks again for your support!

Printed in Great Britain
by Amazon